T5-ANT-782

Pineapple Thoughts

Ja Runyon

Pineapple Thoughts

J.A.Runyen

authorHOUSE®

AuthorHouse™ LLC
1663 Liberty Drive
Bloomington, IN 47403
www.authorhouse.com
Phone: 1-800-839-8640

© 2013 by J.A.Runyen. All rights reserved.

No part of this book may be reproduced, stored in a retrieval system, or transmitted by any means without the written permission of the author.

Published by AuthorHouse   08/14/2013

ISBN: 978-1-4918-0770-5 (sc)
ISBN: 978-1-4918-0771-2 (e)

Any people depicted in stock imagery provided by Thinkstock are models, and such images are being used for illustrative purposes only.
Certain stock imagery © Thinkstock.

This book is printed on acid-free paper.

Because of the dynamic nature of the Internet, any web addresses or links contained in this book may have changed since publication and may no longer be valid. The views expressed in this work are solely those of the author and do not necessarily reflect the views of the publisher, and the publisher hereby disclaims any responsibility for them.

Contents

Book Thoughts

Short statements:

1. When my husband passed away suddenly I found myself numb with disbelief. I needed to find some way to deal with the loss and numbness and found myself exploring my childhood. A childhood where I had been sad a great deal of the time but in revisiting some of my experiences I found comfort in looking back—and hope for the future.

2. One woman's journey dealing with the sudden death of her husband by visiting memories of her childhood. These glimpses of the past reminded her that although throughout life we have to deal with sadness, there are precious moments and tomorrow may bring more unforgettable good experiences. She decided that something she had read once was true: "Live for today, plan for tomorrow, and remember the past with kindness." (Unknown author)

Life can be tart and sweet at the same time and we quite often hide our feelings under a tough skin.

I

Alone

"Why do you have the television on when you are not watching or listening to it?"

Sarah turned her head in surprise, as she had been quite alone a moment before. She was attempting to read a Readers Digest Condensed book and had just one dim light shining on the book and the light from the television to light the room. It was hard to tell in the dimly lit room but she had reached the age where clerks no longer hesitated to offer her the senior discount even though her ash blond hair showed just a few gray hairs. Perhaps it was the fifty extra pounds she carried on her 5 foot, 2 inch frame that gave her age away.

A young girl, eight, ten, (or was she fifteen?) was sitting on the day bed. Sarah felt she should know her, but there shouldn't be anyone here tonight. Bill had been gone almost a year now and her son, Jim, who was staying with her temporarily, was working and wouldn't be home until 2:30 a.m. No, there shouldn't be anyone else here.

Sarah reached up and turned off the television. The young girl said, "Oh, that's much better."

"I feel your presence so strongly, yet I know you cannot be here. Is this what a nervous breakdown feels like? I thought one just became moody and cried a lot."

The girl looked at her, "You have been calling me to come, so I am here, Sarah."

Sarah sat back and said, "Why am I not afraid of you?—For I am not. If this is not real then I just won't tell anyone. I have had very few secrets in my life and everyone's entitled to a few. What should I call you?"

"I think since you called me you should name me."

"Then I will call you Delila. It was my grandmother's middle name. Being a middle name it was not used much, which seems a shame, since I think it is a prettier name than her first name of Alice. The beauty hidden in the middle, just like my grandmother, who never felt pretty but was very good and beautiful inside, in the middle of her being. Delila, why did I call you?"

"Perhaps, Sarah, you were lonely."

"I have been lonely. I miss my mother. She passed away suddenly about ten years ago. I miss my grandmother also, but she's been gone over 25 years. I think I have been missing you too. Why is that? What are you to me?"

"I can't say, but I will stay with you as long as you need me. Thank you for the name, 'Delila'. I knew your grandmother a long time ago."

"Then you must be from my past. Is this magic of some kind?"

Delila smiled and shook her head from side to side as if amused by the question. "You used to believe in magic. Do you remember the hole in the ceiling?"

Sarah smiled, "Back that far? Why I was about four years old. My babysitter's son came home from the war (World War II). He had a little sister about six years old. He had presents in his suitcase. He must have given me some candy or something since I didn't feel left out. He said, 'See that small hole in the ceiling?' (It was about the size of a quarter.) 'I can take one of you girls and by magic push you right through that little hole.' I ran and hid behind a chair so he grabbed his little sister and started lifting her up to the ceiling. He said, 'Go get Mom to see this.' So I ran into the kitchen to get her and when she came back with me, his sister was nowhere to be seen and he was talking to the hole in the ceiling. 'Are you alright Sissy?' I was sure I heard her answer 'Yes'. His mother said, 'You get Sissy down and come to dinner.' Now that was magic."

Sarah just sat there staring ahead then looked at Delila. Delila had a very solemn look on her face. She had small features and blond hair and a sad look in her eyes. Sarah said, "What's wrong?"

With a deep sigh, Delila said, "I felt your sadness just then, what were you thinking about?"

"I was thinking about that babysitter and something that happened after her son went back to war. In back of her house was a huge pile of trees and tree stumps that were being cleared from the property so they could build some more 'defense houses'. These homes were being put together as cheaply and quickly as possible to house all the people working in the shipyards. My mother was a welder in those shipyards and that's why I had to have a babysitter. All the kids in the neighborhood played in that pile of trees and stumps. It probably covered a half-acre. One day I had to go to the bathroom and instead of running home I just squatted down in one of the holes made by the trees and went potty. At four years old I didn't even care that some of the kids saw me. But Sissy told her mother. Her mother put a diaper on me and held me up in the window for all the kids to see and made me stay in and wear it all day. I had been potty trained since age two and I can still feel the humiliation of that day."

3

Sarah looked up and Delila was gone. The room felt very empty.

The next morning Sarah struggled to separate from dreaming to being awake. Her eyes didn't want to open. She alternated from falling back into her dream and finding herself trying to direct the dream to resolve itself according to her wishes. Finally she woke up enough to realize that the dream didn't make much sense. Something about a retirement hospital located in a lighthouse on a small island and she wanted to climb to the top and watch the sea. As usual the dark mood she experienced in the middle of the night was gone. Sarah decided that just like she didn't expect her dreams to always be logical, she could accept her small visitor, Delila, without caring if seeing her made sense. Sarah climbed out of bed and started her day. She went into the kitchen and filled a bowl with cereal and milk, poured a cup of coffee, and took them into the dining room.

Delila was sitting in the window seat with the sun shining behind her. She said, "You used to always eat in the breakfast nook."

Sarah sat down at the table and smiled. It still felt strange to talk to someone who shouldn't exist or maybe wasn't even there, but she knew somehow that there was no evil attached to this small girl. She looked at Delila and said, "Ever since we remodeled the kitchen and put the computer in the nook, it's just not as comfortable. We used to have a table and I used to sit on one side and my grandpa on the other. My grandma sat at the end so she could get up easily to pour coffee or milk or wait on us."

Delila said, "What's wrong? Why did you stop? I like remembering good times."

"I just realized that I never said I missed my grandpa."

Delila looked at Sarah questioningly, "You loved your grandpa." It came out more a statement than a question.

Sarah thought a moment, and then said, "Yes. When I was a child I would have said I loved him best. Whenever I knew I was going to my grandparents, it was always him I was most anxious to see. He was the one who played with me. He told me stories and sang songs, like—'Home on the Range' and 'Clementine'. He also played the banjo, violin, and several sizes of harmonicas. He would put one harmonica on a stiff wire that was around his neck and was bent to hold the harmonica in front of his mouth. Then he would play either the banjo or violin at the same time. My Grandpa made me feel very special. He had a 1939 Buick Sedan and would drive me and my grandma to Cannon Beach to play on the sand by Haystack Rock."

"I loved summer at my grandparents. I had three neighborhood kids to play with: Jackie who was one year younger than me and her sister Jeanine was one year older and their baby sister, Chrissie. They lived two doors over from my grandparents. My grandpa had built me a swing set. He had sunk two 4x4s into the ground and hung two swings, one was rope and one was chain. We used to compete to see who could swing the highest, of course we would always chicken out when the height of our swing caused a slackening of the rope or chain and then made a jerk as the swing came back down. Grandpa built me a merry-go-round teeter-totter. The property used to be a cherry orchard and he had one stump that he had not dug out. He cut it so there was about three feet of tree left. He then sunk a piece of water pipe in the center of it. He took a board that was probably ten feet long and three inches thick and cut a hole in the center. He placed this over the pipe. He attached a T shaped handle on each end to hold on to. With a person on each end you could push your feet to one side as you pushed up and around you would go; up and down, around and around. It was quite magical. My grandpa also built a sandbox around a tree so that when I played in the sand during the heat of the day, I would have shade. He hung a hammock between two trees. I think it was made from chicken wire attached

5

to two sticks. My grandmother had made a mattress like padding to put in it to lay on"

"My grandparents had learned long ago to make do with what they had. They did not throw many items away. My grandmother even took old plastic bread sacks and crocheted them into rugs. There were picture books that my grandmother made by pasting pictures in a scrapbook. She had books of cards that she had received and books of poetry that she had cut out of magazines and newspapers. My grandmother had a trunk filled with old dresses and lace curtains. Jackie (she was the one I played with the most) and I used to play dress-up and the lace curtains made wonderful shawls to wrap around our shoulders and over our hair."

Delila shifted her body on the window seat and turned to sit cross-legged like children do so effortlessly. She looked at Sarah, "That's the grandpa and grandma times that I remember. Why do you look sad?"

Sarah looked pensive, "When I was a young child my grandpa was my playmate. After I got older, he was still there. We just didn't have any real connection. My relationship with my grandma changed over the years, just as I changed. As I got older she told me about her life and I had a more honest picture of their life together. I think my grandpa was a very good grandfather, but not a very good father or husband."

Delila looked sad, "I think I will remember the Grandpa as good. You can tell me about the father and husband part if you want to, but I liked the Grandpa."

"You are right. I was lucky to have my grandparents when I was small. My father was a Seabee in the Navy and my mother went to work in the shipyards so I spent a lot of time with them. I remember just a few things from World War II because I was so young."

"When my father was going to be shipped to the Philippines, my mother and I rode a train all the way across the United States to Rhode Island to see him just before he left. I was just getting over the measles and my parents had to tell the landlord in the boarding house that I had hives from eating strawberries or they wouldn't have let us stay. What I remember of that boarding house was that everyone ate together at a long table and there was a window seat in our room and I sat looking at the snow falling. I begged to go play in it, but since I was ill, I wasn't allowed to. We said goodbye to my father and rode the train back across the United States to Portland, Oregon."

"When I wasn't at my grandparents one of my mother's friends, Iva, took care of me. This was the first family I remember wishing that I were part of. Iva and Ray had two children, Roger (he was two years older than me) and Karalee (one year younger), and a black cocker spaniel named Inky."

"They did things together and I wanted to belong to such a family myself. Iva, Ray, my mother, and some of their other friends used to play cards together. One night I came inside from playing and there was something in the oven. It tasted so good that although I could never remember what it was, I could still remember the taste years later. The closest I have come to the same flavor is JoJo potatoes."

Delila hugged her legs to her chest and laughed. "Oh yes, I know what you mean. That was in the summertime. Summertime was the most fun."

Sarah looked at Delila. "Do you have all my memories? Do you remember when I was five or six years old and we would play 'Annie, Annie, Over'? It had to do with throwing a ball over the house to kids on the other side. One person would catch the ball and the rest would run around to the other side and then the person who caught the ball threw it over the house yelling 'Annie, Annie, Over'. If the ball went sideways over the end of the house we would yell 'pigtail!' We would play this until it was too dark to see the ball, then we would switch to playing 'Run Fox Run', which was really just a game of tag in the dark. The 'Fox' would have to catch all the sheep and then we would pick a new fox and play again." "My mother and I would walk home from her friends house and I would say 'Run Mama, run,' and if she wasn't too tired, she would."

"The years we lived on McLoughlin Heights above Vancouver, Washington were good ones. I had my mother all to myself. We lived in one of the defense houses. I remember it had a stove in it. I can't remember if it was wood or coal. I just remember it was always so cold when we got up in the morning. I was six years old and my mother had to leave for work before it was time for me to go to school, I rode a city bus to school. I must have had the same bus driver each day as I can remember him making sure I got off the bus at the right stop. I was very small for six years old. Mostly I remember standing at the bus stop in the dark and cold and feeling very alone."

When Sarah looked up, Delila was no longer there. She seemed to always go away when Sarah had a negative thought or unpleasant memory.

That night Sarah's restless mind would not let her stay asleep so in the early a.m. she decided to write down her feelings in the hopes that recording them would lessen their impact and allow her to sleep.

Alone

The emptiness, the abyss, is claiming me once again. I feel it coming. Imagine the loneliest place you can, and then multiply that by a million or more.

A deserted island? No, there is beautiful scenery, sun, wind, and rain.

A desert? No, there are living beings all around: bugs, snakes, lizards, small critters and birds. There is the sun and the stars.

The middle of a busy city? Now we are getting close; the loneliness of a million souls bumping against each other and not touching, but even this offers a diversion, something to watch and wonder about. What do these souls truly feel? What do they think about when they are alone? Are they ever alone? Do they run from one activity to another, only stopping to sleep when so exhausted thought is not necessary or even welcome?

No, this abyss does not contain other souls. It only comes when it is dark, usually when I awaken in the middle of the night after struggling with some problem; a problem I can find no solution for; when I feel so alone in my struggle for an answer and no one cares. The emptiness enlarges and I sink into the middle of it, far from contact with anyone or anything. It is dark and quiet and solitary, and I am totally and completely alone—no sound, nothing, nothing, and nothing.

Like the black hole in space—empty.

I am lucky. I seldom stay for long in this black hole of nothingness, but it waits quietly, insidiously, and eternally for me to join it. However, in naming it, I have given it substance and turned it into a tool for survival. When it comes again—and it will—I shall sink into it, reaching for the companionship of emptiness that will give me the strength to reach out ever knowing that the reality I reach for may never connect with mine.

II

Kasey's Paper

"I wish I knew my dad." The voice in Sarah's memory came unbidden from the past as Sarah watched Kasey continue down the street. She hadn't seen much of her grandson in the past few months, as he was very busy at college. She had watched him change over the years into a young man any parent would be proud of.

Her daughter and grandson had lived with her and Bill until Kasey was ten years old. Then they moved to a house on the same block. Kasey had stopped to talk when he saw Sarah retrieving her morning paper from the front lawn. It was just the normal chitchat that families do.

"Hi, you're out early."

Yes, I'm on my way back to college."

"How are things going?"

"Oh, you know, study, study, work, party, study, work, work! I'm getting used to little sleep and long hours. Last year was harder when I first started my part-time job. It was necessary though. College is expensive and Mom's salary can only stretch so far."

"Does your dad help?" Sarah, thought—now why did I say that? It's none of my business; it's just that I know Jenny has raised her son alone, with little help from Kasey's dad over the years.

Kasey didn't seem to mind answering, "He sends some money, but you know my father; it has to be for something specific, not roof over our head or clothes on my back. Well, got to rush or I'll miss my bus. Bye."

It was that statement; "you know my father" that took Sarah back to that day when Kasey was about five years old, before his father had made any attempt to see him. Sarah had been pushing Kasey in his swing while Jenny was inside making sandwiches for lunch.
Kasey put his feet down to slow the swing, and said, "I wish I knew my dad."

Sarah didn't know quite what to say, "You know who your dad is. Your mom has shown you his picture."

Kasey had hung his head and drug one foot in the sawdust, "Yes, but I wish I 'knew' him."

Even fifteen years later the memory of that day brought tears to Sarah's eyes. She indeed did know what he meant. Her own father had left when she was three and had only visited her a handful of times. He died when she was twenty-five and she never had the chance to 'know' him.

Sarah watched Kasey turn the corner ahead and thought, "It's telling that he used the term 'my father', not my dad. Kasey had told her once, 'He's my father, biologically, but he's not my dad'."

Seeing Kasey head off to college made Sarah think, maybe I should take some more classes at the community college. I'll dig out my old assignments and see if my brain still works.

Later that evening, Sarah pulled out her file of school papers from about eight years before when she had taken some classes. In among her old school papers she found a few of Kasey's recent college papers. She was always inspired by Kasey's ability in writing and had saved every piece of his writing that he let her read.

He wrote one of the papers shortly after his Grandpa Bill died of a sudden massive heart attack. After reading it, Sarah turned off the lights and sat in the dark trying to remember the last 45 years with Bill, but her mind wouldn't go there. It was like there was a block on her memory. The only clues she had were in Kasey's paper. She turned the light back on and reread it before going to bed.

Kasey's Paper

William Walter, Bill, Grandpa. There are many names that describe my grandfather for me. He died of congestive heart failure about one and a half months ago. He was a 6-foot, 320 lb man with gray hair and a comb over. My grandpa always loved to wear a flannel short sleeve shirt, Dickie's, Velcro shoes, and his trademark suspenders. I can vividly remember the things he would yell at me in his tool shed, "Kasey, you dumb-shit, you got me the wrong tool," or "How dumb can you get?" These catch phrases of him to me used to mean a lot less to me than they do now. Now every time I think about these moments I just smile and begin to cry. All I can think is that my grandpa was the only sort of father figure I had and now he is gone.

A real clear memory I have of my grandfather and me probably was when I was about ten. My mom worked overtime everyday to pay the bills and keep food on the table for me. My grandpa would always tell me how proud he was of her for supporting me on her own. For this reason, my grandpa became my new ride home from school everyday. He would pull up in his 1987 Ford van: dark brown, with a light brown trim, tinted windows, a bench seat in the back that laid out into a bed, and the coolest horn you would ever hear. A small panel right underneath the stereo controlled it. It had twelve different buttons for twelve different tunes. I always remember the times when my friends and I would play hide and go seek in the gigantic bushes in the front of our school. Everyday my grandpa would wait to see one of us with our backs turned to him and he would hit his number 6 button. It was the loudest, most annoying sound I have ever heard. We would always jump out of the bushes in fear and my grandpa would just laugh.

Another one of our daily traditions was one that probably made me a rather tubby child. Everyday after grandpa would pick me up we would head straight over to his favorite place in life, 7-11. My grandpa went to 7-11 everyday ever since I was a baby.

When the owners of 7-11 heard about my grandfather's death they cried. I really loved that about my grandpa, how he could and would make friends with anyone. Anyway, everyday we would go into 7-11, I would be sent to the back of the store to get grandpa and me each a one liter bottle of Mountain Dew. Meanwhile, he would head on over to the chips and grab each of us the largest bag of Cheetos Puffs he could get. He would always give me the money to pay for the food so that I would feel like a big shot.

When we would get home from 7-11, we would each grab a television tray and sit around and watch cartoons such as Chip and Dale's Rescue Rangers, Darkwing Duck, and X-Men. We would watch cartoons like this until my mom got home around 6 or 7 p.m. This was a tradition of ours up until I moved to Beaverton three years after it had begun. I can still remember the feeling I would get every time I heard that horn go off. It was like when you see a little boy run into their father's arms with that look of satisfaction in their eyes knowing that they are safe now that they are with their dad. I used to get that feeling, and every time I think about my grandpa I realize that he was not just my grandpa, he was my dad. Most people consider their dads to be their fathers. I think that a dad is the one man in your life that cares about you more than any other man on earth. I have a father still, but I have lost my dad.

III

Response To Three's

The following morning Sarah awoke thinking about her mother and then realized she had a new loss to deal with. The Journal entries she made after her mother passed away made her aware that each loss is unique, however, time had lessened the pain of losing her mother and she resolved to try to be patient again while dealing with the loss of her husband.

After breakfast she decided that it was time to clear out some of the clutter that was stored throughout the house. It was a perfect time, as her son was driving a semi truck to Florida and would be gone for several weeks. The basement was full of stored items that had belonged to her grandparents and mother. She carried three boxes upstairs to the dining room, and then decided to have a cup of coffee before starting.

When Sarah came back with her cup of coffee, Delila was once again sitting cross-legged in the window seat. Delila said, "This house is full of memories," pointing at the boxes.

"Yes, but some of the boxes that are stored just hold old receipts and should have been thrown away a long time ago. I'm afraid there may be something important mixed in so I guess I have to look in every box before tossing the junk. Most of this is boring stuff."

"You have been talking about your life when you were little. What do you remember about your grandma and grandpa back then?"

Sarah put an empty box on the table in case she decided to keep anything and started going through a stack of papers. "Well, let's see, just after I was born my grandparents bought this property and they dug down and poured concrete for the basement. They built the garage first so they could store tools and materials. Then they started building the house but had to stop working on the house during World War II because they could not get lumber and other building materials. I found a letter in their important papers stating they could live in the garage until after the war. The deed for the property has all kinds of rules about what they could build and where on the property they could build and even who would be allowed to live here."

"I remember the garage just had black tar paper on it and there was a wooden path so you wouldn't have to walk in the mud. My grandma put curtains on the windows and they had a woodstove for heat. Last week I saw the porcelain pot stored upstairs behind the wall. It has a lid and is what they used for a bathroom facility. It's called a 'slop jar'. I'm sure it was hard for my grandma to cook, wash clothes, and make a home under such circumstances, but I thought it was fun and a kind of adventure. I had some fun times in that garage. I came down with the measles while visiting them in the garage. My grandma made sure to keep the garage warm enough and took good care of me. That was just before my mother and I rode the train across the United States to Rhode Island."

Delila said, "Do you still have that 'slop jar'? It sounds funny."

"Yes, I don't think I will throw it out, although I can't imagine having to use it now." Sarah walked towards the living room. "See this chair." She turned it over and showed Delila how it had been mended with a board on top. Underneath you could see it had a round hole cut in the original seat. "I think this is what they used over the top of the slop jar. Pretty inventive, I think."

Delila laughed, "I can see that you really don't like to throw anything away."

"I'll go get the slop jar. Would you like to see the deed and letter also?"

Delila looked unsure, "Would you read them to me?"

Sarah looked up and realized that this Delila looked to be only about six years old, like she was mirroring whatever age Sarah was talking about. "Sure, they are in a metal box that is upstairs also."

Delila watched her head for the stairway in the living room and said, "That's a different stairway."

Sarah stopped and turned, "The old stairway is still there in the hallway. I just really like open stairways so my husband built this for me. Someday I will tell you all about him if you still come and see me."

Delila looked amused; "I will always be with you in some way."

The box was just where Sarah remembered. She turned from the closet and Delila was now sitting on the hope chest in Sarah's room. "Just a minute, I'll get the slop jar. See, it's just a metal pot with a lid. They used to also call them chamber pots."

After Delila had finished giggling at the thought of actually having to use a slop jar, Sarah opened the metal box and took the letter out. "That's strange, it looks like the letter was to the people that my grandparents bought the property from. This is what it says:"

'The undersigned are not in anyway attempting to vary the restrictions on the property they bought from you, being Lot or Tract 8 of Teeney Place, according to the duly recorded plat thereof in Multnomah County, Oregon, subject to all building restrictions of record.

The undersigned wish to advise you that they desire to live in a garage upon said property until six months after the present war is over, at which time the undersigned shall have started to build a house in accordance with the restrictions that are upon the above described property.

In any event, without regard to the date that will be 6 months after the present war is over, the undersigned will comply with such restrictions within 4 years from the date of this letter, or which ever of the two dates is the shorter.

This is to be regarded as a temporary accommodation to the undersigned and not a waiver of any restriction.'

Delila said, "How interesting. Did people have to do without very many things during the war?"

"Oh yes, many things were rationed. Somewhere in a box I have some of the old ration books. This house is full of history. That's why I hate to throw anything away without really thinking about it. Oh, here's the declaration that is attached to the deed for the property. It's dated: March 1, 1941. I'll only read the interesting parts. There is a whole lot about how close to the property line you can build and that kind of thing." She proceeded to read:

'No noxious or offensive trade shall be carried on upon any lot, nor shall anything be done thereon which may be or become an annoyance or nuisance to the neighborhood.

No Chinese, Japanese or Negroes shall use or occupy any building on any lot, except that this covenant shall not prevent occupancy by domestic servants of such races or nationalities employed by an owner or tenant.

No trailer, basement, tent, shack, garage, barn, or other out-building erected on above numbered tracts shall at any time be used as a residence temporarily or permanently, nor shall any residence of a temporary character be permitted.

No dwelling costing less than $2500.00 shall be permitted on any one of above mentioned lots.'

"It also states that these restrictions are binding until January 1, 1962"

Delila looked very unhappy, "It's sad that people could make such laws, especially about who can live somewhere. I like all people."

Sarah put the papers back in the box and placed the box in the closet. When she came out of the closet, she wasn't too surprised to see that once again Delila was gone.

Sarah awoke that night around 1:30 a.m. and lay thinking about Delila and her desire to see the good side of things, and then the dark side of life crept into her thoughts and she was remembering poems she had read in the past, especially "Three's" by Carl Sandburg, and once again she reached for pen and paper to catch her thoughts.

Response To Three's

I was a young child
When I heard three sad words:
War, Death, Hate
And saw the agonies they created.

I was a little older
And heard the words:
Nazis, Japs, Colored.
Those words that labeled and destroyed.

Then there was:
Them and Us, They and We, Black and White,
The bigotry of separatism.

If we knew the heart of man;
The dreams that flattened and flowed out
From all the disillusionment of life,
Would we still hate?

If we heard the laughter
Of each newborn;
If there could be laughter for each newborn,
Would we then hate?

If we could look into
The eyes and soul of each individual,
Would hate be possible?

If indeed, we looked within ourselves
For the essence of our existence,
Would we then hate?

But time is short
And we are much too busy running from reality.
There is no time to fight
The instinct to hate.

Ah—but what a world it could be,
If the words we learned in early childhood
Would be—Love, Caring, Humanity.

IV

Bump

After a week filled with the normal responsibilities of life, Sarah finally was able to sit down Friday night and pick up the scarf that she was in the middle of knitting. The television was on just for background noise. She was thinking back to her conversation with Delila and her life when she was young.

"Do you remember when the war ended?" The question came from Delila who was sitting cross-legged on Sarah's bed. She was looking questioningly at Sarah.

Sarah reached over and turned the television off and answered, "You always seem to know what I'm thinking. I remember how happy everyone was, especially my grandmother. She said that our boys would be coming home, including my father. It turned out that she was only partly right. My father came home, but he did not stay. My mother said that they both loved me but couldn't live together."

Delila looked pensive, "He did come back for your 6th birthday. That was a fun day."

"Yes it was. My grandmother gave me a big birthday party and all the neighborhood kids came. My mother put curls and a big ribbon in my hair and I wore my best dress. I felt very important. I can remember my mother and father sitting on the front porch talking quietly to each other. I have a picture of them sitting there and my mother does not look very happy. When the party was over they took me to Blue Lake and we rode in a boat. At the end of the day my father left for California."

Delila looked hopefully at Sarah, "He said he would come back to see you."

"I started waiting for him. I kept thinking that any day he would be there. In the meantime, due to the war being over and all the young men coming home, my mother lost her job at the shipyards and had to go back to being a waitress. It didn't pay nearly as much so she decided to move us to North Portland. We lived in a small duplex right next to Pier Park. I spent a lot of time alone. I remember going to a big hill in Pier Park, climbing to the top, then laying down and rolling all the way to the bottom. That rolling feeling reminded me of the feeling I got when, as a baby, someone would rock me; except instead of back and forth, I was going around and around. I don't remember meeting any other children while we lived there. I guess I was very lonely."

As the memory of being lonely crept into Sarah's mind, she looked up and Delila was no longer there. Sarah was a little bit perturbed. Couldn't Delila stand any sad thoughts? Then Sarah thought, "She comes to me as a small child, perhaps she only has a small child's viewpoint."

Losing interest in her knitting Sarah decided to catch up on her sleep. The next time she awoke, rolled over in bed and looked at the clock it was 4:15 a.m. Once again she was awake and reached for pad and pen.

Bump

It is the middle of the night and once again the force of darkness has been calling to me,
The loneliness of nothingness.

This time it did not last long as my mind floated among memories
Exploring the bumping of my life.

Like a bumper car going down a long corridor, bumping against the walls,
Where each bump is a life experience. Bump! Bump! Bump!

I realize that each bumps force is controlled by me
On my side of the wall of this long corridor called life.

I smile—Bump—good Bump—generating a vibration on that wall that perhaps
Someone Bumping on their side will feel, causing their next Bump to be a positive one.

Bump! I Bump against someone else's good vibration and pass it on.
I feel the connection to all of life and my responsibility to pass along good vibrations.

I know in this life as I Bump, Bump, Bump along,
I will sometimes pass on a negative vibration.

I see my purpose in life more clearly.
To try and guide myself down this corridor with no wall scarring Bumps.

Bump! Bump! Bump! Gentle Bumps, a smile here, a kind word there

Give some love for no reason, just because, Bump, Bump, Bump.

It feels good—gentle Bumps—a smile here, a kind deed there,
A belief in humanity, a belief in others, a belief in myself.

Personal integrity does not depend on anyone else's actions, only my own.
Bump! Bump! Bump! Down the long corridor called Life.

V

Hands

Sarah came upstairs from the basement thinking about where to buy some linoleum to cover the laundry room floor. It was impossible to get all the dirt off of the concrete floor and clean clothes dropped on it would no longer feel clean and have to be rewashed. It was just one of many things on her to do list that she had taped to her refrigerator years ago in a fit of frustration. The list had items on it that she had wanted to get done for years but couldn't seem to convince her husband that they needed doing. Now that he was gone, it was up to her.

This need to take action by herself was new to Sarah. She had always wanted his approval before starting projects because he knew how to do so many things. He just knew how things worked or went together. He would hardly look at directions while Sarah always had to go in order: Step 1, Step 2, Step 3. Usually the smartest thing she could do was stay out of the way, just running for tools when he asked. It made for fewer arguments if she just let him do it his way and the result always turned out fine.

Sarah looked at the list on the fridge. Some items had finally been marked "done", but others fell under the category of "probably never".

"Enough negative thinking, just do something, anything, make a decision." Sarah had started talking to herself out loud when no one was around. She had seen older people in stores chattering to themselves and hoped she would at least only do it at home. "Oh well, so I'm a little bit crazy. We used to tease my mother about her "Finlander" comments, when she would say something silly or forgetful. It was part of her charm but we said it was the Finn in her because her parents came from Finland. I've always been so proud of my Finish heritage because when I was growing up every Finish relative was always so nice and kind to me."

Sarah looked over in the kitchen nook and realized she was perhaps no longer talking to herself. Delila was sitting cross-legged, on top of the low file cabinet that sat in front of the window where Sarah's cats liked to sleep in the sun, waiting for Sarah to continue.

Sarah said, "Do you remember Swenson?" Delila nodded, tipping her head in anticipation of a story.

Sarah continued, "The earliest time I remember being in Swenson was when I was very young and my mother took me to visit her father, my Grandpa Hill. I don't remember him from that visit, only a very nice older lady (I think it was my Grandpa's housekeeper) who gave me a sugar cube. I had never had one before and I still remember the way it sat on my tongue before melting into sugary sweetness."

Delila licked her lips like she tasted that sweetness. "Do you remember Aunt Bertha and Uncle Mel's farm?"

"Yes." Sarah started putting some clean dishes away while her mind went back to that visit to her Aunt and Uncles farm. "I couldn't have been much older than eight or nine when my mother let me stay with them for most of the summer. Bertha was her younger sister and her and Mel had three girls; Carol was a little younger than me, Joanie was two years younger than her and

Marla was a baby. They lived on a farm just outside Swenson. It was wonderful.

Delila said, "That was such a fun summer, please tell me about it."

"Well, we turned off the main road near Napa, and went up and down steep hills, kind of like a roller coaster ride, only straight: up and down, up and down. We turned into a long driveway with lots of trees and scrubs along side. The house was back off the road about a half a city block. There was a large field to the right with a big barn and a fence all around. The house had a porch all across the front. You went up about four steps to the front door. The living room was on the left and the eating area on the right with no walls dividing them. There was a doorway off the eating area to the right that went to the kitchen. There was a doorway towards the back from the living room and another from the dining room; behind each was a bedroom. The one off the living room was for the three girls and the one off the eating area was for Aunt Bertha and Uncle Mel. The bathroom was between the two bedrooms and could only be entered from one of the bedrooms. You had to remember to lock both doors so someone would not accidentally walk in when you were there. It was a small compact house but I thought it was wonderful.

I had been alone so much that it was really fun for me to be sharing the bedroom with my three cousins. It was a small room, but the window was open to all the country sounds, like crickets and small animals and birds. The air had a cool sweet smell. Aunt Bertha had glued stars that glowed in the dark to the ceiling so it was almost like sleeping outside.

We spent our days outside roaming around the farm, making up different games to play. We would walk down near the road and hide in the bushes and wait for the "witch" to come up the road. I'm not sure what her name really was, but we called her Mrs. Pumpernickle. She always dressed all in black with a cape around her shoulders and a hat on her head. Poor lady; she really did look like a witch. We always hid because if she saw us she would turn us into something. After she passed by we would take the foxgloves (bell shaped flowers) and try to make them pop or put them in our mouth for the sweet nectar.

One game we played was not so fun for me. It was called "scare the city kid". Uncle Mel had warned me not to go in the fenced area by the barn if I saw the bull out there, because sometimes he was mean. My cousins made it sound like if the bull just saw me, he would break through the fence and stomp me into the ground. For a while I wouldn't even come off the porch, until Uncle Mel (although he did laugh) told the girls to stop teasing me and said, "The bull won't bother you, if you don't bother him." I don't think he knew what to make of this small, shy, mouse of a girl.

Aunt Bertha took us clamming a couple of times. She would wake us very early to catch low tide and we would climb in the car and sleep while she drove us to Seaside to dig for clams. Once we got used to the cold morning air, we would help her find the clams. She showed us how to tamp the shovel handle on the sand to find the clams air bubbles; then we had to dig really fast before the clam dug down deeper to get away from us. Then we would go back home and Aunt Bertha would clean and fry the clams on her wood stove. They were the best clams I have every eaten, tender and flavorful.

I remember Uncle Mel as this strong man with a booming voice and a huge laugh. I was in awe of him. Aunt Bertha was quieter but impressed me because she had time to put stars on her daughters ceiling and to play with us. I wished I could live there always, but when summer ended, it was time to be a "city kid" again. That was one of my favorite summers."

Delila said, "Thank you. I love this memory."

While telling the story, Sarah had been washing dishes. She turned to say something to Delila, but once again she was gone, but this time it wasn't due to sadness but, perhaps, a desire to savor the memory of that summer a while longer.

Perhaps it was thinking about Aunt Bertha and Uncle Mel and how hard they worked on their farm, but the image that woke Sarah that night was the hands of people that had touched her life. She could visualize how hands change as they age and she reached for her ever-present pad and pen to capture her thoughts.

Hands

Fascinating hands: the hands of a baby as their tiny fingers wrap around your forefinger, responding to your touch.

The hands of a small child as they hold yours with a calm assurance of your care and protection.

Hands, the day you realize that the dimples of young childhood are gone and the hint of change and growth has started.

Hands growing stronger, needing you less, as you struggle to keep your own hands from grasping and holding; and at the same time staying ready to help and steady. Trying to keep your hand open and flat, palm up, so that should they need you, there is a safe place to land.

The hand not upright and pushing away or closed and clutching, but just there—in case.

Hands where now the finger tips outdistance yours, both in size and strength, reminding you of the day you looked down, saw your parents hands at the end of your own arm and wondered, "how can this be?"

Looking at your parents hands, now grown older and needing your help just as your children's hands are growing strong.

Like you are caught in the middle of a dance of hands, on going—stretching back to the beginning and forward to eternity.

VI

On-Looker

Sarah looked at the front flowerbed with satisfaction over completing one of those tasks that she tended to put off. She decided that two hours bending over was enough for now and went inside to make a cup of tea. While waiting for the water to boil she realized that she was thinking of Swenson and the summer she had visited her Aunt and Uncle.

"I wonder why that popped into my head? It was probably the smell of the plants and flowers in my flower bed." That thought was followed by, "I wonder if Delila will come again?"

As Sarah walked into the family room she saw Delila sitting on the sofa watching the cats that were sitting on their cat perch looking out the window. Sarah looked from the cats to Delila, "Do they know you are here?"

Delila said, "I don't think so, it was only you that asked to see me. You were thinking of Swenson just now. Is there more that you want to remember about that summer?"

"Well not really the summer but more at the end of it. I think I had been allowed to visit my Aunt and Uncle in Swenson because my mother needed to figure out what do to, money wise. I think she was having a hard time supporting us on a waitresses salary."

Delila hesitated a moment, then said, "Oh I remember, that's the year you lived with your Aunt and Uncle in Portland."

Sarah sat sipping her tea for a moment, "When my grandparents picked me up in Swenson and took me home it was no longer to the duplex by Pier Park. My mother and I were now staying with her sister, Laura and brother-in-law, Dan."

"They had a nice little house in NE Portland. There was a small living room, dining room, and kitchen across the front of the house and two bedrooms at the back with a bathroom between them. My Aunt and Uncle had one room and my cousin, Kathy, who was four years old, had the other. It sounds a lot like the house in Swenson, only it really wasn't. This house had an upstairs and a basement. There was one bedroom upstairs, reached by a stairway in the middle of the house. You went up the stairs and turned to the right and walked alongside the low wall that was on each side of the stairway to a doorway for the room that covered most of the upstairs. This room belonged to my cousin, Bob. He was 18 years old and a senior at Jefferson High School. He was nine years older than me. I was a little jealous of his sister, Kathy, because I always wanted an older brother."

"Finding a place for my mother and me, in this small house, was difficult. They decided on upstairs. As you went upstairs and turned left there was a small space, just big enough to place a mattress on the floor. This is where we slept."

Delila pulled her knees up and hugged them, "Oh I remember. It was a cozy space, a good place to be alone and daydream."

Sarah smiled, "I did do a lot of daydreaming. I was too old for naps, but when Kathy took her nap, I would go upstairs and lay there daydreaming. The other place I liked to go was in the basement. There was a sawdust furnace and one small niche in the basement was filled with sawdust that had to be fed to the furnace for heat. I loved the smell of the sawdust. When it was first delivered, through the basement window, it was still a little damp and smelled like being in a forest. The basement also had a small laundry room and a play area for rainy days."

"My Aunt and Uncle were very nice to me. Again, I wished I could have a family of my own, in a house with a Daddy."

Delila looked up hopefully, "Your Daddy said he would come and see you."

Sarah, with a sigh, realized that this Delila looked to be about nine years old and perhaps would only know the early years so she said, "yes you're right, I was still waiting for my Daddy."

Delila smiled, "Tell me about this new home."

"My Aunt Laura was a stay-at-home mother so she took care of me while my mother worked. She would let me explore the neighborhood if I didn't go too far or stay too long. I think that is when I developed the habit of walking up and down blocks and daydreaming about the people who lived in the houses.

My grandparents had some friends that lived one block over and I had been there once with them, so I decided to find the house again. Mary and Bert Clark were my grandparents' age. They invited me inside and fed me cookies. Mary had crocheted and embroidered covers on the arms and backs of the chairs and sofas. I remember being very impressed with her handiwork.

Another time I can remember walking down a sidewalk near where I lived. I was just exploring the neighborhood. It was a sunny day and I was thinking deep thoughts; 'Who am I? Why am I here?' The world felt kind of foreign to me, like I didn't fit, like I belonged somewhere else. Then in my head I felt another presence, as if someone were talking to me. It was so real. Some may say it was the over-active imagination of a lonely child but

I believed it was real. The voice said, 'you are here because you asked to be here. You could have chosen any time, past, present, or future. You said, give me a time and place that is fairly peaceful.' The voice said that I wanted to live near the end of the world after people had developed a lot of knowledge, but not too close to the end. I didn't want to be on earth at the end. Listening to these thoughts that seemed like a message and not my own thoughts, I got the feeling that I had lived somewhere else, in another form; that this life was only a temporary stop on the way to wherever I truly belonged. That for now, I was right where, I not only was supposed to be; but had actually requested to be. I remember the warm feeling of not being quite so alone."

Sarah sat looking out the window lost in the memory of that day. She turned to see what Delila might say and found herself, once again, alone, but this time not feeling lonely.

Sarah kept herself busy around the house for the next few days. She spent Saturday at her cousin, Kathy's. They were having a barbeque for her cousin Bob's birthday. It was always fun to get together with family and Sarah hadn't even realized she was tired until that evening when she came home. Too tired to concentrate on reading her book, she made a cup of tea and sat there thinking about Bob.

She hadn't seen him more than three or four times since that year that she and her mother had lived with her Aunt Laura and Uncle Dan. Her aunt and uncle were both deceased now and Bob was living in their mobile home, where they had moved in their later years. Sarah remembered how in awe of Bob she had been years ago when he was just 18 years old.

Delila was suddenly there, "Did you see Bob today? I remember him as very tall with dark hair and an important way of talking."

Sarah responded, "I was just thinking of how impressed I was when he was in plays at Jefferson High School. I remember seeing him in two performances; one was 'Arsenic and Old Lace', and the other was 'Jane Eyre'. A few days after I had seen 'Jane Eyre' I went upstairs. I had developed the habit of looking in Bob's room. I think I was a little bit snoopy or maybe just bored and trying to entertain myself. Anyway, that evening I went upstairs and started towards his bedroom. His doorway did not have a door, just two curtains blocking the doorway. As I neared, two hands came through the curtain and a voice said "Woooo!" This was the same thing that had happened in the play that Bob was in. The hands were of a crazy woman who was trying to get the heroine. I shot down the stairs scared to death. Behind me came Bob laughing. His Mother scolded him. He said, 'I was just doing a scene from 'Jane Eyre'. I didn't think it would scare her that bad. I'm sorry Sarah, are you ok?' You see since I was an only child, I wasn't used to having tricks played on me, especially not by a boy. I didn't understand boys at all."

Delila was sitting on Sarah's bed. As Sarah told the story Delila's eyes got big, like she could remember the fear, then a look of disgust, as she said, "Boys can be a little mean sometimes. Of course, he did say he was sorry."

Sarah looked at Delila with a grin, "He just thought of it as a joke. He wasn't trying to be mean. I wasn't always so lucky with boys though. One day I was sitting on the front lawn and two boys came by on their bikes and asked if I wanted to go to the park that was about five blocks away. Aunt Laura gave me permission. After that day the two boys would come by often and the one that talked to me first said I was his girlfriend. One day we went to the park and while we were swinging my 'boyfriend' threw sawdust in my face and ran off. I asked his friend, 'Why did he do that?' He said, 'He doesn't want to have you for a girlfriend anymore.' I said, 'He didn't have to throw sawdust. He could have just said something.' I was really upset and walked home alone, crying and mad. Funny I can't even remember his name now."

When September came I started 4th grade at Vernon School. Once again I was the new kid. My mother took me to school the first day to register, then left to go to work. Since school had already started by then, the office lady took me to my class and I had to stand up front while the teacher introduced me to the whole class while I wished I could just disappear.

By the end of the week I had found some kids that lived near me so I had someone to walk back and forth to school with. Although I do remember one day when I was walking alone on Alberta St. a car pulled up to the curb with four people about my mothers' age and they yelled out the window, 'Hi Sarah.' I went over to the car asking, 'Do you know my Aunt and Uncle?' because I didn't recognize them. They talked to me for a while then started laughing and pointed to the hat that I had on my head. It was embroidered with my name. They said, 'Goodbye Sarah,' and drove off. They didn't know me at all. I don't think I ever wore that hat again.

When Spring Break came we were going to drive to the beach, but that morning I was laying on the couch not feeling well at all. I kept thinking, 'I can't be sick, it's Spring Break,' but finally I had to tell my mother and Aunt Laura that my throat and ears hurt. Sure enough I had the mumps. So instead of the beach, I went to my Grandma's.

One day after Spring Break all the girls in my class were asked to line up. They picked all the ones of a certain height (me included) and sent us to the auditorium to try out for Jr. Rose Princess. We all had to say something, I forget exactly what, but I was so shy I didn't speak very loud so didn't get picked. I was both relieved and disappointed. I never liked being the center of attention but I think I wanted to want to be noticed. No one really likes to be invisible to the world."

Delila looked up, "I remember you were tiny and had blond hair. Do you remember liking school?"

"I guess school was ok. I did like music class. We usually sat at our desks and sang and that was easier because no one was looking at you. I pretended that I sang certain songs to my Daddy, like: 'Red River Valley' or 'My Bonnie Lays Over the Ocean.' I thought if I sing and think of him, he would know and come. Then he would take my hand and we would walk somewhere and everyone would see that my Daddy loved me. I just knew that if I never stopped believing he would come."

Sarah finished her tea and took the cup to the kitchen. When she came back Delila was no longer there. She thought, "Just as well, I'm really too tired to talk, I just want to sleep." Sarah awoke after three hours of fitful sleep. She thought, "Perhaps if I put these thoughts on paper I will be able to sleep through the rest of the night.

On-Looker

I am the On-looker searching for my place.
Feeling almost invisible, does anyone know my face?

I hide, no one sees me.
Do I want to be invisible or should I let them see
The effort living in this world is for me.

It's ok—Life has taught me that I am strong
And love of humanity will right any wrong.

There is darkness and strife
But it is balanced by great glimpses of light,
The light of souls that inhabit this earth now
And have been here before.

They teach me of love.
Its glow is bright to light the way to live each day.

I do not like darkness, hate and bitterness so—
I will not dwell upon it.
It is not welcome here.

I invite love into my life.
See the goodness and let it stay.
It chases darkness away.

I choose and therefore I am, invisible or not, here to stay
And I choose happiness today.

VII

Kenton Hotel

Sarah awoke early the next morning and tried to identify her feelings and the idea that she had felt this way before; a mixture of having lost something that would be irretrievable and an excitement that what was ahead was completely new. Then she remembered that she had been telling Delila about living with her Aunt and Uncle.

"You seem so serious, is something wrong?" Delila was suddenly there and seemed to once again pick up on Sarah's mood.

Sarah shook her head, "No I was thinking about what happened next. The last time I saw you I was telling you about when I lived with my Aunt and Uncle. This is what happened next."

"One evening in May I was lying on the floor playing my cousins record player. It was a 'Bozo the Clown' story that you could follow along with in a book. When it was time to turn the page, a bell would ring. All of a sudden my mother was home and she had a man with her. That's the first time I met Charlie. I showed him how the record went with the book. If I hadn't been so intrigued with the Bozo record, I probably would have been too shy to talk to Charlie. I don't remember seeing Charlie again until after I came back from California.

Delila was sitting in the overstuffed chair in Sarah's bedroom watching Sarah make her bed, "Your Daddy was in California. Is that when you went to see him?"

"Yes. As soon as school was out my grandma, grandpa, and I headed for Stockton, California in my grandpa's 1939 Buick. I think we went down the coast before turning in towards Sacramento. I remember Stockton was very hot and dusty. My father and his girlfriend, Faye, lived in a trailer that was behind their business. The business was in a white stone building with a store in the front and a workshop in the back. The store had rows of plaster figurines for sale. My father and Faye were very artistic and taught classes on how to paint the figures. They also sold some that they had painted. I remember that my father knew how to make the rubber molds that were used to form the figures. The rubber smelled terrible while it was cooking. My father showed me how the molds worked and how to scrape the figures so that they would be smooth. I was very proud of the work that I did."

Delila smiled like she remembered that day, "Did you go anywhere in Stockton?"

"We went out to eat in a Chinese restaurant that my father said was the best in town. We were only in Stockton a few days so didn't have time to see any sights. My grandma was not feeling well and was very unhappy with my father but I was too young to understand why. My father was an alcoholic and my grandma could tell he was still drinking. Also, I took an orange out of the refrigerator and Faye got really angry about it, as the orange was hers. My grandma thought that she was really childish about not being willing to give me a simple orange when she had my father to herself all the time. My grandma was so upset that she made herself ill. I don't know if she had a heart attack but my father called 911 and Faye took me into the shop while the paramedics were there. The next day we started home.

We stopped at a motel and stayed there for two days while my grandma rested. When we left the motel, my grandma seemed

41

to feel better. Instead of going up the coast we stayed inland. My grandparents wanted to show me a special garden in Redmond called Petersen Rock Gardens. It was a garden made of rocks, lots of rocks, petrified wood, lava, and thunder eggs. It was a fanciful kingdom of miniature castles and bridges. I loved it and could have stayed there all day, as there was so much to see. I was allowed to choose some small smooth rocks from the gift store. I was having so much fun I wasn't in any hurry to go home, but all vacations end and soon we were home.

Delila glanced around the room, "Do you still have those rocks?"

Sarah walked over to her dresser and picked up a small wicker basket with some stones in them, "No, but I have collected some since I moved into this house. I call them 'worry stones'. I keep them in this basket. See how smooth they are. These were made smooth in a tumbler but it is possible to find rocks at the beach or in a riverbed that have been worn smooth over time. Rolling these in my hand makes me feel calm and connected to the past.

Delila studied the small basket of rocks, "They are all different colors and shapes. Did your mother like the ones you brought home?

"I don't remember if I even showed them to her. A few days after I got back from California my mother told me that she had married Charlie and we were going to live in his hotel. I was very excited to think that we would live in a hotel. I had only seen hotels in the movies and thought all hotels had grand lobbies, winding staircases, elevators, and bellboys.

My mother and Charlie picked me up one evening from my Aunt and Uncle's home to go live in the hotel. When we got there it wasn't anything like I had imagined. It was a large stone building with a doorway in the middle and a lighted sign right above the door, stating, 'Kenton Hotel'. We went through the door and up 22 steep steps to the lobby. The lobby was painted a dark green and seemed very dark and gloomy. There was a long desk in the lobby and just to the right of the desk was a door.

Charlie opened the door and we walked into a kitchen. He said, 'My bedroom is that way,' and he pointed to the right, 'and the living room is over there,' and he pointed to a doorway on the left.

My mother said, 'We have decided that you can use the couch in the living room for your bed.'

After they made up the couch for me, my mother and Charlie went into Charlie's bedroom.

I lay there in the semi-dark (my mother had left a small light on as I could not sleep without a nightlight) I lay there feeling very disappointed. This was not the grand hotel I had expected. I no longer lived in a house with an upstairs and a basement, but in three small rooms, and none of those rooms were mine. I did not feel like I belonged there at all."

Delila made a small sound and Sarah looked over at her. She seemed even smaller and her cheeks were damp with tears as she said, "I didn't want to make you sad."

Sarah had a tear on her cheek also now and said, "It's not anything that you did, in fact, you comfort me by helping me remember; as tucked in the past are memories of how I learned to cope with all of what life brought me. Thank you Delila."

Delila gave a small smile and when Sarah looked up again she was gone.

That night Sarah awoke with a start; had she been dreaming? What had caused this dark feeling? Oh yes, she had been telling Delila about her life at the Kenton Hotel and she had made Delila cry. She knew now that she did not want to make Delila feel bad about those years, but she needed to look at them one last time for herself, and then put them to rest.

Taking out a fresh notebook, she began to write.

43

Kenton Hotel

I was nine when my mother married Charlie, so it must have been 1949 when I first saw the Kenton Hotel. I can't say that I was impressed. In fact, I was disappointed. I had only seen hotels in the movies and thought all hotels had grand lobbies, winding stairways, elevators and bellboys. Reality was quite different.

The hotel wasn't even on the main level but occupied the two top stories of the main building that was built on the south end of the block. Connected to the north of the three-story main building was a one-story section that housed a jewelry and watch repair and a barbershop. On the main level of the three-story building was a furniture store and small café. In the middle of the front of the whole block there was a doorway with a lighted sign above it, stating; "Kenton Hotel." Inside the door was a steep staircase of 22 steps. I counted them many times in the eight years that I lived there, from 5th grade until I graduated from high school.

I was a small, blonde, skinny little girl and looked younger than my age. I was shy, lonely and imaginative. I spent a great deal of time reading and I suppose I expected life in the Kenton Hotel to be like something out of a book. When I look back on it—it was.

My stepfather leased the two top floors, owned all the furnishings and ran the hotel. I met people, well not really met; *saw people* from all different backgrounds. At first we lived in three rooms, a kitchen, bedroom, and living room. The kitchen door opened into the lobby. There was a door to the hall in the living room and bedroom but both were blocked by furniture and kept locked. Looking towards the kitchen door from the lobby the living room was on the left, right behind the long desk in the lobby, and the bedroom was on the right. They both had doorways into the kitchen. I slept on the living room couch. The room had, besides the couch, a chair and footstool, a glass fronted bookcase, a dresser, and an old oak roll-top desk and chair. (I still have that bookcase and desk in my home today.) In one corner was a small closet with a curtain draped across the opening.

My mom and step-dad would sometimes go out and the night clerk would be my babysitter. I was afraid of the dark and always slept with a night-light, but on the nights they went out I would try to overcome my fear, which was not easy. Remember that curtained closet? Well I had just seen a play of "Jane Eyre" where they had a pair of hands come through the curtain and almost grab the heroine. I would check every corner of the living room, then pull the string of the light over the top of the couch, lie there 30 seconds, turn on the light, look behind the curtain with my heart pounding, then satisfied that all was well, lie down and try again. I would try maybe ten times before giving up and leaving the light on. I don't remember how long it took before I could turn the light off once and go to sleep—weeks, maybe months.

I don't remember being frightened of the hotel itself. As soon as people knew I was Charlie's kid I had a sense of being protected by everyone that stayed there. It was probably a false premise knowing how dangerous the world is today, but it gave me confidence, so maybe it was that confidence that kept me safe. At any rate no one ever mistreated me. The day clerk was a kind, short, heavyset man with a speech impediment caused by a cleft palate. I knew him as "Junior", and to this day I don't know what his given name was. He was always nice to me, but used to say, "This is no place to raise a kid." My stepfather must have agreed because he was very strict.

I had to come straight home from school and usually had some chore to do: dusting or vacuuming the living room, or washing clothes in an old wringer washer that was in the laundry room down the hall. There was a courtyard in the middle of the building on the second floor that could only be reached by crawling through a window. This is where I hung the clothes to dry. I used the window that was in the lady's restroom. The restroom was down the hall and used by all female tenants. Each floor had a men's and lady's restroom. All the inside rooms looked out on the courtyard and I was told to hang the clothes quickly, not look in any windows and be as quiet as possible. Later Charlie taught me how to hand wash the lace curtains that hung in every room and put them on a curtain stretcher. That and once in a while scrubbing the hall and cleaning the bathtubs were the only hotel related chores he asked of me. There were two small rooms on each floor with only a tub in them that all tenants took turns using.

The hotel was basically for pensioners and single adults. We had a few families stay there over the years when they were having financial difficulties, but it was a hard place to bring children because there was no place for them to play. There were single rooms (no cooking allowed) and housekeeping rooms where there was a kitchen and bedroom. The tenants with housekeeping rooms were provided with a change of sheets and towels but were responsible for doing their own cleaning. The maid made the single rooms up daily. She made up the beds, changed sheets, swept and mopped the floors, dusted and picked up litter. Each room had a sink that she would scour. Some tenants were very neat and seldom home to make a mess, and others were real packrats. Charlie would have to contact the packrats every so often with an ultimatum, "Get rid of some of the stacks of newspapers, etc, or the maid will do it for you."

On some occasions when the maid was ill or just didn't show up, my mother would fill in. I would sometimes follow her around, not so much to help, as just to visit with her while she did the rooms. Sometimes there would be pictures stuck in the mirrors that were over each dresser. I would try to figure out what the relationship was to the tenant. If there were pictures of children, I always wondered if he was their father and had to travel to earn a living or if he was divorced.

Besides pensioners, we had many alcoholics living in the hotel. Charlie was an alcoholic himself and had great patience with these people as long as they did not cause trouble or become too filthy. I learned that there are many, many kinds of alcoholics. Charlie was just a periodic kind. He wouldn't drink at all for a long time, then take one drink and not be able to stop for two weeks and sometimes ended up in the hospital. He was rather pleasant when drinking, just liked to talk a lot and was very generous. If my mother had not taught me that it was wrong to take advantage of someone in a drunken state, I could have had a great deal of pocket money during those episodes.

Charlie was a stern, opinionated, stubborn Welshman, but I truly believe that he was the best thing that could have happened to the Kenton Hotel. He had integrity, loyalty and high standards. He was very intelligent and understood a lot about human nature. The hotel had a reputation during World War II of being a serviceman's delight for one-night stands. I never saw that type of thing while I lived there. Charlie did not stick his nose in other peoples business, so I suppose if they were discreet and paid for a room he would not press them for proof of marriage. However, I don't think he would have tolerated anyone coming in night after night with someone different.

Charlie would sometimes carry someone on the books for months if he thought they were trying and some of the tenants who had been there a long time never had their rent increased. One that comes to mind is "Boston Blackie". He was stocky, had black hair and a mustache. Somehow that mustache made him seem mysterious. He always paid on time, was quiet and had the room next to Charlie's bedroom. He was only asked to change rooms when Charlie felt he had a room available that Boston Blackie would like as much as the one he was in. When he finally moved down the hall, I had my very own bedroom.

I had a door out into the hall and could also enter Charlie and my mother's bedroom by going through her closet. My room had a fire escape. I used to dream about sneaking out in the middle of the night and going down the fire escape. However, I never had the nerve since the last part of the ladder had to be lowered to the ground, I guess by a persons' weight. I probably didn't weigh enough to make it move. However, I did use that door to the hall to steal down the back stairway to the side street early in the morning when everyone else was asleep. I would go for walks and after Kenton Park was built, sit in a swing and daydream. I would always try to be back before anyone woke up and if they were awake I would just pretend I had gone down the hall to the restroom.

I can still see the pattern of the linoleum on that hallway. It was groups of flowers and I used to step from one group to another in a kind of sidestepping dance. I looked at that pattern when I was happy, bored, and miserable, as one of the places I escaped to be alone was that restroom down the hall. I always had to do the dishes immediately after dinner and my favorite delaying tactic was to go down the hall to the restroom. My step dad was onto me of course, but most of the time he let me get away with it, as I knew better than to stay too long.

The toilets were old fashioned with the water box on the wall almost up to the ceiling and there was a pull cord to flush with. The lighting was dim, both in the restroom and hallway. It gave out kind of a somber feeling that usually matched my mood.

I wasted a great deal of my youth feeling sorry for myself. I felt I had a mother, grandmother, and grandfather, but no home and a father too far away. My real father was in California and I only saw him every few years. I always received gifts and cards on special occasions but I wanted to be someone's little girl and Charlie left absolutely no doubt that I would never be his little girl. "You have a Daddy, don't call me Daddy." Looking back, although he denied the title, he did parent me. He kept me safe and held up strong standards of behavior. But I will tell any mother or father, a child cannot have too much love and approval. If a child has a stepparent, great, hopefully they get lots of love from that stepparent, but if the non-custodial parent does not give them love also, they will always feel incomplete. I was taught to love my real father, but I mourn to this day the fact that I never truly knew him or he never knew the real me. He is now deceased. I was taught to understand that he wanted to be with me but just couldn't. I was 50 years old before I finally admitted to myself that he was no different than so many fathers today. They have a child and move on, out of sight, out of mind, no feeling of responsibility for how that child evolves, or how much aching and longing there is for that child to feel important to a part of themselves; their own fathers. My father did not value me or he would have been there for me.

I occasionally visit in my heart and memory that little girl at the Kenton Hotel, when times were simpler. When an argument between two drunks meant a couple of fists hitting at each other and not knives or guns. I remember when the horse races were running the jockeys and trainers would stay at the hotel. One time I heard a commotion in the hall and upon opening my bedroom door, saw two very inebriated men tussling down the hall; too drunk to really harm each other. The night clerk, Doc, who was over 6 ft tall, was trying to quiet them down. I never saw Doc be physical with anyone, in fact I think he was a bit timid and if things got too far out of control he'd just call the police. That night the two "fighters" were more an annoyance than dangerous to themselves or others. Anyway, I was watching down the hall when I realized there was someone in the doorway of the room directly across the hall. I was about 13 years old, but looked nine. It was one of the jockeys standing there in his jeans and no shirt. When he noticed me across the hall, he did the gentlemanly thing and went back into his room and put a shirt on. It was such a chivalrous thing to do and made me feel quite grown up. The fight didn't last long and we all went back to bed, but I still remember the jockey with good manners.

At Thanksgiving Charlie liked having turkey with all the trimmings, but with only three of us, it made for a lot of leftovers. He started buying a huge turkey and inviting anyone who didn't have family to join us for dinner. He would set up a buffet on the lobby desk and everyone could have a home cooked meal with all the traditional foods, including pumpkin pie.

I now have a great deal of respect for my stepfather, a stubborn, opinionated, Welshman with a good heart and high principles. He deserves to be remembered for all that he contributed to the tenants' quality of life at the Kenton Hotel.

VIII

Night Sounds

The next morning Sarah sat drinking her coffee and thinking, "I think I could tell Delila some stories. I did have some fun times, times that I wish kids today would have."

Sarah felt a presence, "Hi Delila, did you come for a story?"

Delila grinned and settled into her cross-legged position that Sarah wished she could still do, "You had fun that first summer that you were at the Kenton Hotel."

Sarah thought for a moment then said, "Yes, I guess I did. It was all so new. Charlie didn't know what to do with me after my mother left for work in the morning and told me to go outside in the sunshine, but not to go too far and be back by noon for lunch. I can remember the feel of the hot sun and walking a few blocks looking at the businesses along Denver Avenue: barbershop, jewelry store, small café, furniture store, an ice cream store, liquor store, drugstore, grocery store, Doctor's office, movie theater, and several bars. Coming back down the street and thinking that it was too early to go back to the hotel (after all I had been told to go out in the sunshine) I decided to go into 'Bob's 24 Flavors'. It was on the corner next to the hotel. I didn't have any money. I was just curious. It was a small store, kind of like a 7-11 or Plaid Pantry.

It had some groceries, like bread, milk, and pop. There were magazines, newspapers, and a whole section with rows of comic books. There was penny candy and (of course) twenty-four flavors of ice cream. It would be my favorite store for quite a while. This was before television and reading was my favorite pastime. I loved comic books, especially, 'Little Lulu, Donald Duck, Uncle Scrooge, Daffy Duck, and Nancy and Sluggo. It didn't take me long to discover that Bob would let kids come in and read the comic books as long as they were quiet, careful not to tear the pages, and didn't get in the way of his paying customers. After that day I would often go to 'Bob's 24 Flavors' just to get out of the hotel for a while. This is where I met Kathleen. After talking to her in the store a few times, she invited me to her house. She lived west of the store at the other end of the block. When I was allowed out of the hotel that summer, I was either, at 24 Flavors or Kathleen's house.

It was a small house with a small covered porch at the front. I always had a shiver of anticipation when I went up the steps. Kathleen was my first true friend. She was the same age but always seemed so sure of herself and could think of fun things to do. She had a mother, father, and two sisters; "Beanie" was older by about five years and "Birdie" was two years younger than Kathleen and me. I don't remember seeing very much of her parents. It was almost like they were raising themselves. The mother, Mary, worked as a bartender and was either gone or asleep. The father, Vernon, worked on ships and was seldom home. Beanie, being a teenager, wasn't around much either. It was kind of like my own 'Neverland' with no adults to boss us. Charlie and my mother didn't know that there were seldom any adults around or they probably wouldn't have allowed me to spend so much time there."

"Of course, I didn't spend so much time there when September came. I started 5th grade at Kenton School and once again I was the new kid in class. Kathleen and I were in different classes but at least we were able to walk to school together. Kenton School is on Lombard Street two blocks east of Denver Avenue about 10 blocks from the Kenton Hotel. There was a bus stop right across the street from the hotel where the buses turned around and headed back to downtown Portland but neither Charlie nor Kathleen's folks thought it was necessary for us to ride the bus. Charlie said, "You have two perfectly good feet: use them."

Kathleen was a good student but I struggled, especially with the multiplication tables. Vernon School (the school I came from) would cover multiplication tables in 5th grade. Kenton School had already covered them in 4th grade. I went through grade and high school and never did manage to remember the multiplication tables. I was too shy to ask my teachers for help. Also, it wasn't until my father came to visit when I was thirteen that I got my first pair of glasses. I was extremely near-sighted and had been squinting at the blackboard for years.

I remember liking my fifth grade teacher and I was fascinated by where she kept her handkerchief. She had a large bosom and would tuck it between her breasts. I thought, 'When I grow up maybe I'll be able to do that too.' Sarah grinned and looked at Delila, "Not a good thing to wish for. Smaller is definitely better when you are past fifty."

Delila giggled and kind of ducked her head in embarrassment, "Did you like all your teachers?"

"I think so. Some of them made more of an impression on me than others. My fifth grade teacher (handkerchief lady) was grandmother like. My sixth grade teacher was young and pretty and new to teaching. The whole class loved her. We had another older teacher for seventh grade who was an American Indian. She was very strict. If you did something wrong she took you out into the hall, backed you up against the hot steam heater and lectured you. I remember once during a film, kids were untying each other's shoelaces and she caught them. Out in the hall they went to hear a lecture on fooling with each other's clothing. We all went around for a few weeks saying, 'It was shoelaces!' and shaking our heads in disbelief. However, she was a good teacher. I was always a good reader but she made math make sense and helped me learn how to spell.

"In seventh grade we also had a science teacher who used to spend whole periods reading 'Winnie the Pooh' to us. He was especially good with doing different voices. I think he would have preferred teaching English."

"I also had a social studies teacher in seventh grade who assigned sections of 'Thanatopsis' by William Cullen Bryant. The part assigned to me made such an impression that I have been reciting it to myself 2-3 times a week ever since I learned it. 'So live, that when thy summons comes to join the innumerable caravan which moves to that mysterious realm, where each shall take his chamber in the silent halls of death, thou go not like the quarry slave at night, scourged to his dungeon, but sustained and soothed by an unfaltering trust, approach thy grave, like one that wraps the drapery of his couch about him and lies down to pleasant dreams.' I think that was the first poetry, other than nursery rhymes, that I had been exposed to."

School was ok but after school was better. Kathleen, Birdie and I would walk home. I walked as slow as they would let me, suggesting different streets to walk down; anything to delay arriving home because on most school nights I wasn't allowed to go out once I got home. I would be told to go in my room (I finally had my own room after several years of sleeping on the sofa) and read or do homework. Even after Charlie bought a television I was not allowed to watch very many programs.

Delila interrupted with, "Oh, I remember the first television you saw. It was downstairs in the furniture store."

Sarah closed her eyes and thought: What does Delila know and how does she know it? I think I will have to allow her to return to where she belongs soon before my grasp on reality disappears entirely. But for now I'll just enjoy her positive outlook.

Sarah looked over at Delila, "Yes, they put the set in the window and each evening when the station came on the air, people would stand on the sidewalk and watch the magic. Sometimes they would stand there and watch the test pattern and wait for programming to start as the television station only aired part of the day. I would beg to go downstairs for just a little while in the evening to watch along with the other people. I was very excited when Charlie bought his set."

"On weekends when I was allowed to stay up later and watch the station go off the air, Charlie would have us stand at attention while the station played the National Anthem. We would all stand there with our hands over our hearts. The National Anthem was played with the last image on the screen being a flying American flag and then the screen would go to the test pattern and then black. Charlie said no matter where you where when you heard the Anthem you should respectably stand and be quiet. He was born in Wales but had become a naturalized citizen and very much appreciated what America had done for him.

Delila smiled and her eyes sparkled as she thought of the beginnings of television, "If you couldn't watch very much television, what did you enjoy doing?"

Sarah thought for a minute, and said, "Always I was happiest when I could go to Kathleen's. I remember the first night I was allowed to stay overnight with Kathleen and Birdie. Kathleen's room was upstairs in the attic. It wasn't really a room, just an open area around the stairwell. There was a wooden railing around the stairway so you wouldn't fall into the opening. It was quite rickety. We would walk on top of the railing and hold on to the ceiling pretending we were gymnasts on a balance beam. There was a mattress on the floor in front of a low window. We slept with our heads towards the window and woke up to the sweet smell of rain and the top of our heads damp. We snuggled down under the warm blanket and told each other stories until we drifted back to sleep. It reminded me of Heidi's room in her grandpa's cabin. "Heidi" was one of my favorite books. I wanted to sleep in that room, under that window, every night; but of course my bed was in the Kenton Hotel.

Delila looked thoughtful, then said, "I remember the story of Heidi. Your grandpa reminds me of Heidi's grandpa." Sarah had been looking out the window at the sunshine and when she turned to respond, Delila was gone.

Sarah decided it was time to clean out the flowerbed beside the driveway. It was really just dirt and weeds so she took a shovel and dug out all the vegetation hoping that the weather would be dry for a few days so she could plant some flowers, however when she went in the house, the weather forecaster said that there would be rain tonight and it would continue for several days. It hadn't begun to rain when she went to bed so she was hoping the weatherman had been wrong.

It was still dark when Sarah awoke to the sound of rain. She lay listening to the drops drumming on the roof and thinking about all the times rain at waken her. Not being able to go back to sleep, she picked up a notebook that had some of her writings in it searching for her last musings about rain at night.

Night Sounds

I roll over and force my eyes to focus on the glowing digital red numbers . . . 3:34. The covers are pulled up to my chin and only the cold of my nose indicates that the first signs of fall have arrived. I lay in the darkness trying to separate sounds. I hear nothing unusual, just traffic sounds; like waves of surf crashing on the beach, becoming louder, then receding as the traffic flows past my bedroom window.

The house sits above the freeway and the cars used to bother me until I realized that the traffic passing by sounded like surf, especially when it rained. I love rain at night. I sleep on the second floor so I feel safe in leaving my window open. The sweet smell of dampness adds to the illusion of surf.

I look at the ceiling and something flashes across my vision of darkness, like someone was waving a flashlight outside my window. I strain to listen for sounds of a ladder striking the side of the house or tin snips parting screen. Trucks pass by spoiling the illusion of a sea outside my door, and then I hear a siren and realize what the flashes of light are. I see a regular pattern of red then yellow hit my ceiling like the flash of light from a lighthouse. The surf quiets as traffic slows.

I roll over with relief, the fear evaporates from my throat and mouth as I realize that the coast guard of the city has slowed the storm outside my window and any shipwreck is in good hands.

IX

Fuzzy Logic

It looked like the rain was going to continue all week so Sarah decided to clean out her closet, but first she would have to go to the store and replenish her groceries. Her children dropped by often and she wanted to be sure and have food that her grandchildren would eat. It was always nice to see them but the quiet times were nice also. It gave Sarah time to adjust to the realization that for the first time in her life, she could make a decision without consulting anyone. She was discovering that being alone was doable and some days quite desirable as it gave her time to think about the past.

Sarah carried the grocery bags into the kitchen and realized that Delila was sitting in the kitchen nook looking out at the rain. "The back yard looks like a park. I remember you liked Kenton Park."

Sarah smiled, "Yes, I even liked Kenton Park before it became a park, or at least while it was still in the planning stages. That first summer most of the houses had been torn down but the trees, bushes, sheds and garages were still there. The area was about 12 acres and looked very different from now. The park is now mostly flat with just one lower area where there is a baseball diamond. At that time two of the streets that ran through the park area went down and back up making a valley in the middle. There were only trees, shrubs, and old sheds left and it felt like that area was out in the country. On the west side of this area very few of the streets had curbs. It made the streets feel like country roads. I thought of all the area beyond the west side as out in the country and loved to walk along the roads listening to the birds and feeling free of the city. I would go through the area that would be a park and walk the streets and roads beyond that area a lot, especially when I couldn't find anyone to play with. I looked at the houses as I walked by, wondering what it would be like to live in a house like a real family with a mother and father."

Delila turned away from the window, watching Sarah put the groceries away, "You were able to live in this house sometimes."

"You're right and at that time this was considered way out in the country. My life at the hotel and at my grandparents was very different. At my grandparents house I was their little princess, given total attention. At my home in the Kenton Hotel I was taught to draw as little attention to myself as possible. My mother's favorite expression seemed to be, 'It's not worth making a fuss over. You can do or have it later, or next time.' I lived in a hotel so I couldn't have friends over. I had to depend on them having me over so when I met Kathleen I kind of put a death grip on my relations with her and her family. That fact makes it all the more amazing that I would give up playing with her and the other kids in the neighborhood, but I did. It happened later that summer. We used the planned park area as our playground, exploring all the old sheds and empty foundations, playing hide and seek, cowboys and Indians, and war.

One sunny day my grandma and grandpa drove by the park area just as we were all heading to Kathleen's house. My grandma called me over to the car. They weren't staying. They had just dropped off something that I had forgotten at their house. However, my grandma had a request. When she saw the park area it reminded her of a dream she had just had. She dreamt that something bad happened to me in a wooded area with old sheds.

She said the park area looked like her dream. She asked me to promise her that I would not go into that area again. This was a woman who would do anything for me, so I promised and that was the end of my playing in that area until the park was finished. I would not break my promise to her. I missed a lot of fun that summer and gained the reputation of being a goody-two-shoes. I'm sure there were times later that I carried my goody-two-shoes routine a little far but I'm still proud that I kept faith with my grandma."

"When the park was done it was mostly a flat grassy area with that one area that dipped down. The baseball diamonds and trees would come later. The trees that are there now were just twigs then. On the far Westside there were swings, slides, a merry-go-round, and a wading pool. Later they put up a small building for restrooms and storage and would have park attendants in the summer who would teach us to make craft items, such as plastic gimp key chains."

"They did leave some of the big fir trees to the north of the swings. We spent many a Fourth of July celebration sitting under one big tree watching the fireworks being set off in Vancouver. When I think of spring days and hot summer nights and the smell of grass, I thing of Kenton Park and the people I knew then. There was my best friend, Kathleen, and her younger sister, Birdie, who lived just east of the park. There was Kathy who was lucky enough to live right across the street to the south. She was also the first girl that I knew that was allowed to shave her legs. I remember in the summer she wore shorts and showed off these smooth tan legs. She was not a skinny runt like me either; her legs were nicely shaped. I was really envious. My mother said twelve was too young and that once you started the hair grew back darker and thicker. My mother never did shave her own legs. She was 100% Finish and very blonde so it wasn't really noticeable, but I'm only ½ Finn so I think my leg hair was thicker and more noticeable. At least I certainly felt that way then."

Sarah had finished putting the groceries away and headed upstairs. When she reached her bedroom she wasn't surprised to see Delila sitting cross-legged on the bed. "I remember lots of kids, boys and girls."

Sarah laughed, "All the kids that lived around there would be at the park at different times but of course we liked some of them better than others. I managed to develop a crush on a different boy each year. Not that I remember most of them paying much attention. I was too shy and quiet. There was one boy, Tony, who was two years younger than me and lived in a house right behind the hotel. I never thought of him as boyfriend material, more like a younger brother, so I was able to relax and just be myself. One year, when I was around 11 years old, he broke his leg and was in a cast up to his hip for most of the summer. His mother took the summer off work to stay home with him. I went over every day to play cards and board games with him. I remember it was a very hot summer and the rest of the kids were at the swimming pool. Tony's mother would thank me for being there but I didn't feel like I was sacrificing anything. It felt good to be needed and to connect with another human being. This was before television sets were in every home so we spent the summer in Tony's backyard under the trees and an umbrella, drinking lemonade, eating cookies, laughing, joking and playing games."

Sarah was busy pulling clothes out of the closet and when she turned around Delila was gone. The rest of the day went by quickly as she divided the clothes into piles designated: throw away, keep, and give away. All the time Sarah was thinking about why she kept calling Delila to visit and at the same time hoping this wasn't a sign of dementia; after all she couldn't be real.

She placed paper and pen handy as waking in the middle of the night had become a habit. She wasn't surprised when she opened her eyes and read the clock: 3:33 a.m.

Fuzzy Logic

I have moments of great clarity and moments of fuzzy logic.
It is during the moments of greatest clarity that I see things
with kindness.
The fuzzy logic just brings memories of pain and loss.

Every soul is born with the possibility of being good
And the longing to love and be loved.

My world that I have pulled in around me like a warm blanket
on a cold night
Makes me feel safe.

Do I dare face the chill of "out there" away from my safe haven or
Am I destined to stay in this cocoon only reaching out
cautiously to test the outer air?

Does it hold hope in the form of the warming sun of human
kindness?
Can I share my small corner of existence, helping others reach
for their destiny?

I remember a poem: "Let me live by the side of the road and
be a friend to man"

It seems to me that is what I should do.

X

Jantzen Beach

As soon as Sarah woke up she turned on the TV to catch the weather forecast. The weatherman said, "Rain to continue for at least two days." Sarah thought, "Good, I can put off some of the outside work and spend some time with Delila."

She had hardly set her cup of coffee on the dining room table when Delila was in the window seat. Delila looked out the window and said, "Do you like the rain?"

Sarah took a sip of coffee, "I like all kinds of weather as long as it doesn't stay one way too long. I like hot, hot weather, rain that comes down hard for a short period, and soft rain that comes mostly at night while I am warm and cozy in bed. I even like thunderstorms and snowstorms."

Delila looked thoughtful, "I remember snowstorms and school being closed."

"Schools did close sometimes, but I can remember going to school during snowstorms as Charlie would only let me stay home if the radio said school was closed. I think that there is a better system of communication now so the news gets out faster. At least when it was snowing Charlie would let me ride the bus; especially the year we had the big snowstorm. We got on the bus at the turnaround (across the street from the hotel) and the bus headed up the hill. The power for the buses (they ran on electricity) was in overhead lines. There was a bar on the top of the bus that reached up to the line. The snow and ice would make the bar disconnect and the bus driver had to keep getting out of the bus to pull on some ropes that were attached to the bars and reattach the bars to the line. After about 45 minutes of only going four blocks we gave up, got off the bus, and waded through the snow the rest of the way to school.

The weather was so bad that the school called a snow day but made everyone who had made it to school stay until in the afternoon when the storm died down. The school was closed for the next few days. Of course, we spent those days playing outside in the snow.

We went sledding by 'Suicide Hill'. It was such a steep hill that if you weren't careful enough to turn at the bottom you would be propelled right across Columbia Blvd. There wasn't as much traffic on Columbia Blvd back then, but there was enough to make it very risky to cross on a sled. However, that is not why it was called 'Suicide Hill'.

Sometime before I moved to the Kenton Hotel, some kids were playing under the cliffs (that were beside our sledding hill) digging into the hillside making caves and the dirt collapsed trapping them. I think three kids were killed.

I had to promise to stay away from 'Suicide Hill', and I sort of did. I only went on the sledding trail that was to one side of it. Of course, I didn't tell Charlie or my Mom exactly where it was that we went sledding.

Delila looked a little surprised, "I thought you always tried to be good and not get into any trouble."

Sarah smiled, "I was kind of a goody-two-shoes type of kid, but even I did some sneaky things. I was like all kids in that I never thought anything bad would happen to me so going sledding next to Suicide Hill didn't seem wrong."

Delila seemed to be intrigued, "What other sneaky or bad things did you do?"

Sarah thought for a moment, "I think I may have done some wrong things by accident but I can only remember three times that I actually stole something on purpose and I only felt guilty about one of them. The first item was a calculator that belonged to my cousin, Bob. The day we were leaving to move to the Kenton Hotel I went in his room and took it. I had been playing with it often and I was fascinated by how it worked. It was made of metal, a little larger than a deck of cards, only thinner, with holes for each number. I figured out how to add by putting a pencil point in a hole and pulling it down. I think I only took it because it belonged to Bob and I thought he was the smartest, most talented person. I just wanted to take a piece of him with me. Strangely, I never felt guilty about taking it.

The second time I took a 10-cent comic book from a drug store in Kenton. That was the time that I really suffered. I just knew that the owner would take one look at me and know so I walked on the other side of the street for about six months. If my mother wanted to go in there I would make some excuse to go down the street to the 5 & 10-cent variety store. I decided that crime does not pay and never did anything like that again.

The third time I stole $5.00 from Charlie to go to Jantzen Beach. For some reason I felt justified. All those years I had given money back to my mother when Charlie insisted I take it during his drunken sprees; all those years I had heard from my mother 'you can do or have it next time, it's not worth making a fuss'; I think I thought, 'just this once I'm going to do what I want.' I did and I never felt guilty.

Delila inquired, "Jantzen Beach? The amusement park?"

"Jantzen Beach represents my childhood. It was wonderful. My grandparents took me there when I was very small to the picnic areas where the Carpenters Union had their annual picnic. There was a small train that wove all around the park and I rode it each year. I also rode the Merry-Go-Round. My grandparents showed me the building where there used to be dances that they went to when they were young. When I moved to the Kenton Hotel, Jantzen Beach was just a mile or so down the road. At least a few times during the summer all the neighborhood kids would walk to Jantzen Beach to swim. There were three pools. The deep one had a tower to jump off of. I never did but my friend Kathleen was braver than me. Heights have always bothered me . . . There was one pool that was too shallow to dive in, but there was a fountain on one side and it was safe for beginner swimmers. The third pool was just a wading pool. We used the wading pool when we were cold; since it was shallow it warmed up fastest. There were grassy places to put our towels and lay in the sun. There was a snack bar. We would pool our money and share French fries. If we paid for swimming we never had enough to do all the other activities in the park. There were rides: Roller Coaster, Ferris Wheel, Octopus, Tiltawhirl, Carousel, and some I can't remember the names of. There was a haunted house where you sat in a car that was on a track that went inside through the dark, where things would jump out at you and cobwebs would hit your face. There was a fun house with a crooked room, a walkway where people could see you out front and air would blow your skirt up if you weren't careful, and a barrel that would tumble you over if you went inside it. There was a tunnel of love with boats that floated on water and lovely scenery. It also was very cool on a hot day. We would let our boat get inside then hold on to the wall until the next boat bumped into us. We never did use it as a 'tunnel of love'."

Delila said, "I seem to remember one summer when you spent a lot of time at Jantzen Beach."

"That was the summer that Charlie and my mother were separated. I don't remember exactly why. It could have been because of one of Charlie's drinking binges, or dealing with me,

65

or just getting used to being together. Anyway, my mother was a waitress at Waddles (right across the street from Jantzen Beach) so she found a small duplex on Hayden Island right behind Waddles. It was at the end of seventh grade so I must have been almost 13 years old. We moved there just before school was out so I took the bus each day. When school was out my mother let me go swimming almost every day. I think she thought it was a safe place for me to go and she would know where I was. By the time school started in the fall, my mother and Charlie had made up and we moved back to the Kenton Hotel."

Sarah glanced out the front window and was surprised to see the sun just poking out from behind dissipating clouds. "It looks like the weatherman was wrong," she said as she turned to where Delila had been sitting a moment before and found herself talking to air. "Oh well, I guess I'll clean out the Gazebo and pick up the yard."

By nightfall there had been one brief shower followed by a few fluffy clouds left in the sky so Sarah wasn't surprised when the weather forecast changed to "Clear skies and warmer weather ahead."

Sarah's last thoughts that night as she drifted off to sleep were about Jantzen Beach and that one summer.

She awoke in the morning very slowly with visions of the past and lay there savoring the memory before reaching for pen and paper.

Jantzen Beach

I went to bed very late; after 1:00 a.m., so I awoke at 8:30 a.m. this morning very slowly with visions of my past.

I am alone. It is a sunny day, just like this morning. It must be about 10 a.m. and I am walking through the gate at Jantzen Beach Amusement Park. There is no admission fee this early because most people that come this early just want to go to the swimming pool for lap swimming. Instead of turning to the left toward the pools I proceed straight ahead past the huge white wooden roller coaster. I am about 12 years old and no one pays any attention to me. It is like this is my private playground.

I walk past the small square booth where there is cotton candy. There are just a few people around getting their booths ready for the crowd of people that will come later. Some are checking their inventory of prizes, or drinking coffee, or reading a paper. The candy apple booth smells sweet as the vendor dips apples in red coating or caramel sauce. I mentally set aside fifty cents to buy one later.

As I walk by the games of chance I think, "Should I try to pop a balloon for a prize or fish out a boat from the circular moat?" The boat will have a number on the bottom corresponding to a number on the board showing what I can win. I will not spend any money, just yet. I want to savor the sights, sounds, and smells of my private park. This is the one time that it is nice to be almost invisible. No one yells at me to, "Come on, give it a try, and see what you can win!"

As I walk along, to my left is the Tilt-a-whirl and Octopus; to the right is the Haunted House. I save the Haunted House ride for days that are so hot that riding in a car on tracks through the swinging doors into cool dampness is a relief from the relentless heat, with the added thrill of being safely spooked.

At the end of this wide aisle is the Fun House. I will probably go in there first. There are so many parts to explore that it helps stretch the little money I have. I can spend up to an hour inside. I climb up ramps to a crooked room where there are railings to hang on to as gravity seems skewed. In a lower area there are giant drums that when I enter tumble me around like I am a gem that needs polishing. On a slanted area are discs with poles through the center. I hold onto the pole with my feet on the disc and lean until gravity pulls me around to the lower side and if I do it just right I can go faster and faster around, similar to pumping a swing only using my weight and arms to pump instead of my legs. I go to the top area where the front is open so people can watch from outside and be enticed to enter also. There is no one to see me this early. I push between the huge soft mattress rolls that are turning, step onto the silver discs that turn in different directions trying not to grab the railing, then across the clacking wooden bars that drop like a teeter totter, left and right, as I step on them. I scurry across the area where air shoots up even though I am wearing shorts and don't have anything to blow over my head.

I come out finally and turn to go to the carousel, walking past the Tunnel of Love, where boats wait to carry riders through the snake shaped dark tunnel, past lighted scenes. I only ride on a boat when I have several kids with me. We like using the ride to escape the heat, usually upsetting the operator by stopping the boat inside until another boat catches up with us.

As I reach the carousel I look for my favorite horse that will propel me up and down as the Merry-Go-Round turns. I allow myself to spend money on a ride. As the attendant helps a father and small boy (no one else is on the ride) find just the right horse, I think, "Someday I will ride with my father," and then I climb on my horse, hold on tight and just enjoy the motion.

After the ride I decide to walk back past all the booths and maybe eat something before I go swimming. I know I won't buy anything to eat; it's just an excuse to experience my private park before all the people show up. If I had continued around through the picnic area I would have reached the pool sooner. This way by the time I retrace my steps and turn toward the pool I will really appreciate the cool water.

I pay to get in and rent a towel. I have my swimming suit on already so I just slip out of my shorts and top, lock them, with my shoes, in the locker and pin the key to my suit. I splash some water on me in the shower (as little as possible) then wade through the disinfecting pool to the outside. I take my towel and place it on the grass near the snack bar. I will retrieve some money from my locker later after I have played in the water and soaked up heat in the sun. I look in both pools for familiar faces, or at least someone my age. Swimming, wading, splashing is more fun if there is more than one person. I don't think being almost invisible is a good thing at a pool.

The sun relaxes me and I remember that I am hungry and thirsty. I buy some French fries and a snow cone. I soak in the sun some more, checking the clock on the side of the building periodically. I want to leave enough time to buy a caramel apple or cotton candy before starting home.

XI

Darkness

The weather report had been for, "warmer weather ahead," and summer finally arrived with temperatures in the 90's. Keeping the windows closed kept the main floor of the house in the mid 70's, but the second level needed a window air-conditioner just to make it cool enough to sleep.

The heat kept Sarah home and she had no company as her family and friends only went out if work required it. Except for a phone call or two, Sarah was alone. She had little energy for projects so spent the days reading or puttering around the house. One day she found a box on a shelf in the basement took it up to the dining room and started sorting through it. She found a story that she had written when she was seventeen.

Sarah was deep in thought and somewhat startled when Delila said, "You look so far away."

Sarah looked up at Delila who was sitting cross-legged in the window seat, "I haven't seen you in awhile."

Delila smiled, "You haven't needed me or I would have been here. What were you just thinking about?"

Sarah took a deep breath, "Summers in Kenton and going berry and bean picking. Kathleen, Birdie, myself, and other kids from the neighborhood would sign up for strawberry picking just as soon as school was out. A platoon leader would pick us up in a school bus and drive us to different farms around Portland that needed pickers. We would get up very early, around 5:00 a.m. and be out in the fields by 6:30. We would usually be back home by around 2:30 in the afternoon. The mixture of dust, heat, and strawberries created a sweet warm feeling in my nose. In my memory it smells like childhood.

When strawberry season was over we would pick green beans at a farm next to Colwood Golf Course. When we had our lunch break we would go through a small swampy area between the bean fields and the golf course and spy on the golfers. We liked working in the bean fields, as the owners were very good to us. Several times when the day was especially hot they would treat us to a watermelon feed.

The thing I remember most about summer was that we tried to spend as much time outside as we could. When we weren't picking something, we went swimming or to Kenton Park, or just hung out in Kathleen's back yard. I remember one night we were sleeping in her backyard and it rained about 3:00 a.m. It was one of those warm summer rains. We ran over to Kenton Park and splashed in the puddles that dips in the grass created. We got soaked but it was so warm that we didn't care.

Delila pointed at the papers in Sarah's hand, "What have you found?"

Sarah looked pensive, "This is a story that I wrote when I was seventeen. I think this is the first time that I put my thoughts on paper to help me understand life."

Delila tipped her head inquiringly, "Will you read me the story?"

Sarah looked at the title, "June 1956", and started reading:

"It was a rather hot, dusty afternoon as the group started for the bus. There were about 56 strawberry pickers in the group, most of them children and about six grownups. They were leaving behind them a field clean-picked, mostly because there hadn't been anything to pick in the first place. Some wouldn't be back the next day; others would come because of a promise of better berries. Some were just out for a good time and still others had no choice. If they wanted spending money, they had to work.

The bus driver, Denny, led the way. He was a young fellow of about 20 years of age, inexperienced but conscientious. Why just last night he had the bus checked because the gears were hard to shift. It was an old bus they had gotten this year and there were a lot of jokes about the way it rattled and shook. Still it got them to the field and back the first day and probably would the rest of the summer.

Right behind Denny flocked the kids. They were of all ages ranging from nine to nineteen. Coming along a little slower were the two ladies that came picking for extra money. There were always a few older people every year and out of courtesy for their age, seats were reserved for them on the bus.

Behind them quite a ways walked three figures: Mr. Randaul, Mrs. Randaul and Julie. Mrs. Randaul was the platoon leader and took a group out every year. She must truly have liked children for during the winter she taught grade school. She was a strangely wonderful person who could put up with a great deal of nonsense and fooling around without becoming angry.

Delila interrupted, "Strangely wonderful? What did you mean?"

Sarah thought back to those days, a little sadly, "I think my experience with adults was that most of them liked children to be seen and not heard, so it seemed strange to me when Mrs. Randaul was so patient."

Sarah continued with the story, "Her husband, Mr. Randaul, was checker for the group. He made sure that everyone received credit for what they picked. He was very strict with his son, Bobby, but a visitor in his home was always treated with courtesy.

Julie was sixteen and a friend of the Randaul family. She walked with them instead of with the kids so she could talk with them for a few minutes and help carry anything that Bobby might have overlooked. By the time the trio reached the bus, almost everyone was seated and ready to go.

The bus was over-crowded today because Mrs. Randaul had taken a rather large number of pickers from another platoon. However, squeezed three and four in a seat, everyone managed to get seated although one boy had to sit in the doorway. Julie sat between Mr. and Mrs. Randaul in the seat right behind the driver. Every once in a while she would trade with Mr. Randaul, who was on the aisle, so he could relax a little.

They were going over the hills towards Hillsboro when Julie noticed that Denny was watching the temperature of the engine quite closely. Looking at it she discovered why, the temperature gauge only went to 200 and it was already on that. Julie was tempted to ask Denny to stop the bus and let the engine cool off but she didn't. After all, what did she know about engines?

They climbed another hill and the engine seemed to be cooling off. Then the bus started down the other side. Everything was all right until suddenly Denny said, "The brakes are gone!" Mr. Randaul jumped up and tried to help him put it in gear. It hopped out of every gear they managed to put it in. Before the bus picked up speed they could ditch it, but that would more than likely kill the boy sitting in the doorway. They couldn't do it. It would have to be something else. All the time the bus was picking up speed. It was going faster and faster. They came to a slight turn and managed to make it. Denny and Mr. Randaul were talking and it seemed like time crept, yet all the time the next turn was coming, a steeper turn that the bus would find impossible to make. They decided to go straight out across a field. Mrs. Randaul stood up to tell the kids to sit down. Half of them didn't know anything was wrong.

The plan of Mr. Randaul and Denny was simple; drive into the field where the soft dirt would slow them down and by driving around a clump of trees, head up hill enough to stop the bus. Only one thing went unnoticed. At the roadside in front of the field was a deep ditch. When the bus struck this ditch, the speed with which it was traveling jackknifed it causing it to flip end over end three times.

Just before the impact, Julie told herself to relax completely. So instead of trying to hold on Julie just put her hands in her lap and sat there saying the Lords Prayer, which was the best thing to do under the circumstances. As the bus hit, Julie was thrown into the air; the dust rose so thick from the floor that nothing could be seen and she closed her eyes. It was just like being tossed around in a big barrel. She didn't seem to hit any sharp objects but she was aware of contact several times. There were screams, not blood-curdling, but of alarm that this was happening to them. Everything was confusion when the bus landed upside down.

Julie found herself within the bus pinned by her left arm between the top of the bus and a window casing. She tried to pull loose. She couldn't; all she could do was pray. There was a nauseating odor of gas. She yelled for someone to get her out. She heard people talking outside: "There's someone still in there." Who is it?" "It's Julie." "Is that you in there Julie?"

Then Mr. Randal tried to get her out. She seemed to be caught by her blouse sleeve. It looked to her like her arm was half cut off.

Denny kept running back and forth checking to see if the ignition was off. Mr. Randaul yelled at the boys not to smoke near the bus. There was a little boy across from Julie caught by his fingers. They finally got him loose.

Bobby came to the door just as she asked, "How is Mrs. Randaul?" She hadn't seen Bobby there but he answered, "My Mom's dead." She told him to go away—if the bus should catch on fire—one in the family was enough.

Tony, a good friend, stayed with her most of the time and helped her keep hold of herself. He said later that he thought she had been swearing but what she had said was, "Oh, dear God", over and over again.

Two men from a farm nearby came and tried to help. They told Julie to pull when they lifted. The first time they lifted, she screamed because it had put more pressure on her arm instead of less. It seemed like hours, in reality it was probably only 5 to 10 minutes, before she finally could pull free.

Fear is a strange thing. It was a fear that the bus would catch on fire that enabled her to have strength to pull free. When she got out of the bus, she discovered herself much luckier than she had thought. She had only scraped the skin off her back and badly bruised and pinched her arm.

Tony led her away from the bus toward the middle of the field. He had a bad cut on his head and finger. He had crawled out of a window after the bus landed.

Julie sat in the field pulling at the young blades of wheat. They were soft and tender and the sky was blue.

Later in the hospital Bobby was running around checking on everyone and making jokes. It seemed like he either didn't believe his mother was dead or was trying not to think about it. There were a few people with injuries but Mrs. Randaul was the only one to die. Julie felt a great loss and resolved to never forget this day.

When Sarah finished reading, Delila was gone.

The heat kept Sarah up late waiting for her room upstairs to cool down. She finally went to sleep and was perturbed to find herself awake at 4:00 a.m. She tossed and turned and finally gave up. She picked up her pen and started writing.

Darkness

The Nothing is here again.
I speak its name and I feel something deep inside.

It is a call to arms; I will not give into this dark mood.

Just speaking it's name; just giving it a name—
Gives the mood substance; something I can fight.

I am and always will be stronger than
Anything that tries to diminish my spirit,
Because once a long time ago I prayed for help and strength

And it came day-by-day, minute-by-minute.
Just keeping on keeping on,
One foot in front of the other.

I feel love in the air.
I try to take my lessons from the people I see
That have shining spirits.

Some have names because what they are is so exceptional:
Mother Theresa, Christopher Reeves, Mattie Stepanek.

Others have small moments, but they all humble me.
The dark mood lifts.

It was not important.

XII

Grief

The next afternoon Sarah was folding towels and trying to decide what to fix for dinner, although she really wasn't hungry. It was too hot. She could go to the neighborhood buffet but she didn't eat enough to make it worth spending $9.00. She thought, "Too bad Nohlgren's $.99 All You Can Eat isn't still in business."

Whenever Sarah started dwelling on the past Delila usually appeared and sure enough there she was sitting in the window seat, "What happened after the bus accident? Did you go berry picking again?"

Sarah looked at Delila and thought, "I'll bet she knows exactly what I was thinking about", and then she answered her, "No, Charlie decided it was time for me to get a real job. His timing was terrible because one of the boy's in the neighborhood, Ron, had invited Kathleen, Birdie, and me to go to the beach with him and his parents. Charlie said "No". So while everyone else went to the beach I applied for work at Nohlgren's. It was a 99 cents all you can eat restaurant. I was hired as a dessert girl. I would scoop up dishes of ice cream and cobblers hour after hour. That was my first job with a weekly paycheck. I liked it alright but I would have rather gone to the beach."

Delila seemed lost in thought, and then said, "You said you didn't feel guilty for taking $5.00 from Charlie. Did you like him?"

Sarah looked sadly at Delilah, "No, in fact until I was grownup and married with children I would have said that I hated him. It's sad because now that I am older and can evaluate him as a complete person I have let go of the anger and feel love for him. He was whom he was because of what life had taught him and what he believed to be true. He had a daughter who was five years younger than me. She lived with her mother and rarely visited us. I was old enough to want a sister but we just never seemed to connect. I think at first she just wanted to be home with her mother and later was perhaps jealous that I got to live with her father. She need not have been jealous. I only called Charlie "Daddy" once. He told me, "I am not your father, you have a father in California. Do not call me Daddy." That hurt so badly at the time but I think he was thinking that he didn't want his daughter calling someone else Daddy. He truly believed that "blood" was what was important and I was not of his blood.

He and I never connected and the sad thing is that I don't remember him trying to. I felt tolerated and controlled but not loved. Of course, maybe I was buried too deeply inside myself for our two personalities to have a chance to connect. I spent too much time wishing things were different and longing to be loved.

Sarah looked at Delila, "I'm sorry. I didn't mean to make you sad. I found someone to love when I was nineteen. Would you like to hear that story?"

Delilah looked up and nodded her head, "Yes please."

I didn't know it, but the direction of my life started on that hot summer day, July 1st, 1958

After I had graduated from high school a year before, I moved from my mother and stepfather's home to live with my grandparents. Birdie convinced me that I would never grow up if I didn't leave my grandparents home so I moved in with her. I had been living with Birdie and her Dad for a few months trying to become more independent.

Moving to Birdie's house seemed ideal, since her father worked at the shipyards and was seldom home. It was the two of us batching it, but without the strain of rent or utilities to worry about.

On that summer day, we decided to go over to the park that was just across the street from her house. It was one of our favorite places to just hang out, sitting on picnic tables or swinging and talking. We were half way across the park, headed for the play area, when we saw a young man walking towards us. As he got closer we recognized him. I had never gotten over the huge crush I had on him two years ago when he was dating Birdie's older sister, Kathleen.

He had the bluest eyes, dark hair with a curl that dropped down on the middle of his forehead, and thick "Peter Lawford" eyebrows, drawn together, that gave him a dangerous rebel look.

As we approached him, we waved and Birdie said, "Hi Bill, remember me, I'm Kathleen's sister and this is Sarah."

Bill smiled and replied, "Sure I remember you Birdie. How have you all been?

Birdie filled him in on our living arrangement and told him Kathleen was living on her own and working for the Credit Bureau. "What are you doing in town? The last we heard you were in the Army."

He lit a cigarette, took a long drag on it and said, "I'm just home on leave, but I'm thinking of not going back. I've got a sergeant who's a real jerk."

I looked at him, and in my usual "goody-two shoes" attitude said, "You can't mean it. That would make you AWOL and don't they put you in jail for that?"

He just laughed and said, "Yeah, probably, but I haven't made up my mind yet. Well I got to go. I'm looking for some old records and Orval said he had some. I like the old songs."

Not wanting to let him go without some future plan to meet, I said, "My grandparents have lots of old records. They even have an old windup phonograph."

To my delight and relief, Bill said, "Why don't I come over later and we can go out to your grandparents."

And thus started the rest of my life, with an AWOL soldier with dangerous blue eyes who was as troubled in his way, as I was in mine, both of us coming from abnormal families.

Sarah looked at Delila, "So, you see I did find someone to love."

Delila eyes danced at she responded, "Oh yes, I remember. He seemed so sure of everything and I remember that he did not go AWOL and he loved you back."

Sarah picked up another towel to fold and looked at the window seat. It was empty. She stood there thinking for a moment then walked into the living room and picked up the memory book that her daughter had put together after her husband passed away.

It was filled with 45 years of pictures of him. Sarah took her coffee and the book out to the Gazebo. She looked through the book, stopping to smile as she came to pictures that evoked memories of those years.

She finally put down the book thinking, "It's ok to remember the past. My conversations with Delila have helped me through this year. I think I'm almost ready—she left that thought hanging for a minute—ready for what? . . . Whatever life brings."

When it was bedtime Sarah took a fresh notebook and placed it by her bed. She knew she would continue to write in the middle of the night because that was when she gave up control and just let the thoughts flow. At 3:45 a.m. she reached for the pen and paper.

Grief

I am learning to wait.

I have not been a patient person.
When an idea presents itself to me I usually want it "right now".

Life has taught me that I am seldom going to get anything "right now",
But I still want "right now".

When my husband died I wanted to grieve "right now" and be done with it.
It doesn't work that way. My feelings were frozen with disbelief.

Now my feelings are starting to flow just like a frozen stream.
It is becoming the springtime for my emotions.

It is all good because even though there is pain,
There is also joy because my heart wants to remember all the good.

So on days when a sharp shard of ice breaks away and I feel loss
I also feel blessed because I feel love towards all in my past who are now gone.

I am beginning to expect nothing from them "right now" except good memories.
The bad has been washed downstream and is like a drop of water in the ocean of life.

The Love remains.

XIII

Coastal Prayer

The first year anniversary of her husband's death came and then the second year went by. Sarah started to enjoy her own company and life fell into a pattern. Sarah had read that one should avoid making any big changes after losing a loved one. The experts said, don't sell your home or move out of town, and don't change your job or make any large decisions for at least one year or more.

Sarah was already retired so changing jobs wouldn't happen and she loved her home and didn't want to live anywhere else. Still she needed a buffer from the reality of how her future had changed, so she remodeled the bathroom and then the kitchen. Her family made sure she stayed busy and visited often for the first year after her husband died. She and her sister-in-law, May, (who had lost her husband five months earlier) met up at least four days a week for the first nine months. They explored all the stores and shopping malls in the area. They went to the casinos and left a little money and they also loaned money to their families.

As time went by Sarah's children still visited but not as often. She and May still saw each other but usually only twice a week. Once for shopping and once to meet at the "Pig N Pancake" for breakfast.

Then one day Sarah noticed that she hadn't had any visits from Delila for quite a while. She realized that she wasn't thinking about her childhood but was more focused on now.

Spring came and May and Sarah decided to go to the beach for a couple of days. They felt they deserved a little holiday at the casino on the beach. They gave themselves strict limits on how much they would spend. They had both made the mistake of overspending for the last two years and were budgeting carefully now.

The slot machines were kind to them and allowed them several hours of playing before keeping the budgeted gambling fund. Lunch was at their favorite little restaurant on the beach. After lunch Sarah decided to take a walk on the sand and May had a book she wanted to finish. They walked back to their room. May settled into the large overstuffed chair by the window to read while Sarah grabbed her beach bag to carry water, a small blanket, and her ever present notebook for writing thoughts in and headed to watch the waves. It was one of those perfect days; blue skies with a few fluffy white clouds and no wind.

Sarah spread the blanket out on a log and proceeded to enjoy the view. She remembered other days at the beach with her husband and children. There was a family walking along the shore and a small girl came running back and calling to her parents to hurry and come see some treasure that she had discovered. This brought Sarah's thoughts back to her own childhood. She felt a warm, happy feeling and looked up and sitting in front of her was Delila, picking up sand and letting it run through her fingers.

"Hello, Delila. I haven't seen you in a while but I haven't been lonely for you. I wonder why that is?" Delila smiled, "I told you that I would always be with you in some way, so you cannot miss what you have not lost."

The wisdom in the eyes of this small girl seemed ageless and Sarah smiled back at her. "I love you, Delila. You are tucked safely in my heart."

Sarah and Delila sat watching the waves roll onto the sand and Sarah sensed before looking over that Delila had left. She knew that she would continue to have small moments of bittersweet memories, the kind that sometimes bring tears, but she would always remember the small girl with the big heart and know that all children deserve to be valued.

After Delila disappeared, Sarah sat looking out to sea, then picked up her notebook and started to write.

Coastal Prayer

I must go down to the sea today to wash away hurt, anger, and shame
In the waves of gentle persuasion.

I must feel the sun warming my heart and soul
To reach for my own salvation.

I need to walk on the hard sand and have the sea come gently in
And bring the salty water over my feet
Reminding me of the taste of tears of regret and sadness
Hoping the sea will cleanse my soul.

I need to walk in the soft sand where life is hard
To build strength for the future,
So as to be able to fulfill whatever destiny life has for me.

I need to look out over the seas of time hearing the lessons of life
In the sound of the surf
And know others have walked here too.

How many multitudes have stood and looked at this horizon
Hoping, wishing, praying for knowledge, strength, and forgiveness?

It makes me feel alone and connected to all of life at the same time
Knowing others have walked this way in sorrow and joy for centuries.

May I connect with those who stood here before
And hear their message of courage, hard work, and love
And learn to give as they did.

To be reminded of those that I have met in my life who give
As automatically as they breathe in and out
Knowing no other way to live.

I want to be that way too.
I will let the sea teach me.